Fundamentals for the Academic Liaison

ALA FUNDAMENTALS SERIES

ALA FUNDAMENTALS SERIES

Fundamentals for the Academic Liaison

Richard Moniz, Jo Henry,
and Joe Eshleman

**Vincennes University
Shake Learning Resources Center
Vincennes, In 47591-9986**

An imprint of the American Library Association

Chicago   2014

Printed in the United States of America

18 17 16 15 14   5 4 3 2 1

Extensive effort has gone into ensuring the reliability of the information in this book; however, the publisher makes no warranty, express or implied, with respect to the material contained herein.

ISBNs: 978-1-55570-967-9 (paper); 978-0-8389-1988-0 (PDF); 978-0-8389-1989-7 (ePub); 978-0-8389-1990-3 (Kindle). For more information on digital formats, visit the ALA Store at alastore.ala.org and select eEditions.

Library of Congress Cataloging-in-Publication Data
Moniz, Richard J.
    Fundamentals for the academic liaison / Richard Moniz, Jo Henry, and Joe Eshleman.
        pages   cm. — (ALA fundamentals series)
    Includes bibliographical references and index.
    ISBN 978-1-55570-967-9 (alk. paper)
    1. Academic libraries—Relations with faculty and curriculum. 2. Academic librarians—Professional relationships. 3. Academic librarians—Effect of technological innovations on. I. Henry, Jo. II. Eshleman, Joe. III. Title.
    Z675.U5M5755 2014
    027.7—dc23   2013050031

Book design in the Melior and Din typefaces.
Cover image © Terence/Shutterstock, Inc.

♾ This paper meets the requirements of ANSI/NISO Z39.48-1992 (Permanence of Paper).

ALA Editions purchases fund advocacy, awareness, and accreditation programs for library professionals worldwide.

Contents

Preface

The role of the library and librarians on campus has changed dramatically in the past two decades. As most librarians are well aware, the library is no longer viewed as an isolated warehouse of books and the librarian no longer seen as a disconnected player in the higher education workplace. Despite prognostications to the contrary, the library and librarians remain as relevant as or perhaps even more relevant than ever before with regard to the academic enterprise. Since the adoption by the Association of College and Research Libraries of information literacy standards, the transformation of the Internet from its days as a static resource into the fast-changing, interactive environment that most of us depend on reflects the new normal. Librarians must come to see themselves as much more integrated than in the past. The services performed and the educational role played by the library staff are what really makes a difference. Attending college is one of the most important decisions that one makes, and it is the total college experience that makes it so valuable. This is something hard, if not impossible, to replicate by Massive Open Online Courses (MOOCs) and similar efforts to relegate teaching and learning to some sort of rote, prepackaged activity. Teachers can still add enormous value to the learning process, as can librarians. We wrote this book because we believe that library liaisons are at the forefront with regard to the future of library services in this technological age.

Our modern culture is clearly conducive to an approach to life where one plugs in headphones to one's iPhone and tunes out the "real world." One communicates not in thoughtful face-to-face discourse but rather through texts and tweets limited by character counts and through the often trivial nature of "discussions" on Facebook. We are not Luddites. In fact, our book will touch on many of the exciting and innovative technologies that can be used to enhance and improve the role of the library liaison. A library liaison's role is to act as a link or bridge between the library and faculty, staff, and students. Through this connection the academic liaison provides support and information on library resources and services to further the overall academic mission. Our contention is that much of what needs to be done by liaisons is best done, at least initially and when possible, in person. The establishment of relationships with the faculty they serve is the cornerstone of good liaison work. We will cover much in great detail in this book, but if forced to boil it down, we would say that this is the goal—establishing genuine and useful relationships with others. Interpersonal skills are at a premium and must be the focus of our overall intent.

As you read through our work, we hope that you will get ideas and be spurred on to consider new approaches and avenues for building and sustaining relationships with faculty. The writing of this book certainly forced us to consider our relationships and what we were doing or not doing well. Improvement in this regard is an iterative process that requires continuous implementation, assessment, and reflection. In our journey we have had the good fortune to work with a number of interesting colleagues. Without the input from and interactions we experienced with others, especially faculty, we would not have produced as comprehensive a work. We owe much to these colleagues as well as our friends and families for being supportive and encouraging. We would also like to express our gratitude and appreciation to college and university administrators who recognize the critical role played by library liaisons. The success of the liaison position is often predicated upon their overall understanding and appreciation for this role and what librarians in general can do in order to enhance the overall college experience.

In closing, and as you begin to explore our work herein, you are reminded yet again that library liaisons are necessary, in fact critical. Do not take yourself too seriously, but always remember that your role as a liaison is one that is fundamental not only to the academic enterprise and to the goals of all of our institutions but also to the students themselves, as you prepare them to live full, active lives with the information skills necessary to be successful in whatever they choose to do.

Faculty/Staff Orientation Meetings

*Fall brings the arrival of a new academic semester, and for the academic liai-*son this means he or she will be giving library orientation meetings for faculty and staff. The library may have new holdings, database offerings, and services. Perhaps a computer lab has been updated or new spaces for group study created within the library facility. Maybe the new library website has been launched over the summer. The library liaison must quickly become familiar with all of these changes and include them in an orientation presentation. This individual is the link between the library and the college's or university's faculty, support staff, and administration. The liaison is also the expert on everything library related. Preparation is important because this is an especially critical time for establishing relationships that will lead to the long-term success of the liaison and the library overall.

Establishing an early connection between the library liaison and the faculty and staff is at the core of liaison work. Without this interaction, an academic library is limited in the assistance and services provided to these personnel. The library becomes an afterthought to the educational experience as opposed to being a fully integrated component of a student's education. A successful liaison program needs a wide variety of interactions. The relationships established with faculty as well as support personnel such as administrative assistants, academic advisors, program developers, and other nonlibrary staff will enhance the library's role in achieving the overall goals of the academic center. Liaisons also can provide critical assistance to faculty, support staff, and administration in other ways (such as supporting research and scholarship). It all begins with establishing a personal relationship, and the first connection will be the orientation meeting.

Advanced Planning Basics

Each college or university is unique, and the orientation meeting must be tailored to serve both the institution as well as the attending audience. Understanding the goals of both the library and the institution is essential. How does the library fit into the overall educational objectives of the college or university? How does information literacy fit in as a component of broader curricular goals? Is the meeting for a community college or other type of institution that has a high number of new professors each term? How will the orientation change if delivered at a well-established college or university where most faculty members and staff have been working for years? Understanding the organization will help in making the decision of what to include and emphasize in the orientation meeting. With this information, it is possible to establish the objective of the orientation meeting. This is the first step.

As a presenter, you must do several other essential things before the orientation begins. If there is a budgetary component to holding the meeting, you must obviously plan out any costs well in advance. If you do not have direct access to a budget, this may require some thought before meeting with a library administrator as to the specific needs. This may not be a factor with a short, thirty-minute presentation, but some orientation meetings may include food, drinks, prizes, or other giveaways. Next, you should determine a location, date, and time. In some cases the library may be incorporated into a broader institutional plan for orientation. Rooms and necessary equipment should be reserved in advance. Along with deciding on the necessary meeting space you must estimate the number of attendees. This is also important to know if information packets or handouts for attendees will be prepared in advance. If the meeting has a food or snack component, the number of attendees is usually required. (Often the approved campus vendor needs a final head count forty-eight or more hours in advance to properly prepare.) Because of these needs, you should set a deadline for the orientation that gives enough time to put everything in place. It is worth noting that an RSVP or sign-up process is ideal but faculty returning from a summer break may be overwhelmed. Accounting for attendees can be challenging but made easier if orientation is mandatory. By chatting with an academic department chair or by looking at the past institutional history of attendance at these sessions, you could be better prepared. Decide how the meeting will be announced and advertised. Again, is this orientation part of a larger faculty meeting that day? Will it need to be on the agenda of departmental faculty meetings or should reminder notices be sent by e-mail? Advertising should be part of the preparation. Remember, as part of this announcement the dates, time, location, and any attractive perks (such as food or giveaways) should be noted. See figure 1.1.

FIGURE 1.1
Advanced planning checklist

FACULTY/ACADEMIC STAFF ORIENTATION MEETING

Assigned Liaison: _____

Date: _____   Time: _____   Location: _____

☐ New Staff/Faculty   ☐ Returning Staff/Faculty

Objective: _____

Budget Allowance: _____

Action Checklist

☐ Room reserved

☐ Equipment reserved/secured

☐ Meeting advertised

☐ Attendees reminder/confirmation notice sent

☐ Number of attendees estimated

☐ Food/beverage ordered

☐ Giveaways secured and organized

☐ Second attendees reminder sent

☐ Handouts printed

Once the advanced planning is under way, it is then time to prepare for the presentation itself. While the orientation meetings will differ between organizations, some commonalities can be applied to any situation. These essentials will be combined in a variety of ways to form the core of the presentation.

Advanced Planning Checklist

- ☐ Objective
- ☐ Budget
- ☐ Location
- ☐ Date/time
- ☐ Advertising
- ☐ Food/beverage
- ☐ Prizes/goodie bags
- ☐ Equipment/materials

Presentation Essentials

Delivering the orientation will also require planning and preparation. There are specific topics of information to cover during new and returning faculty, support staff, and administrative orientations. However, other essential elements of the presentation apply to all audiences. These elements include the presentation medium, staff introductions, food, giveaways, handouts, and the possibility of a physical or virtual library tour.

The medium selected for presentations at orientation meetings may vary. This decision will be influenced by the presenter's preference as well as the actual location of the orientation meeting. In many cases, these gatherings will not take place in the library but in some convenient meeting room, classroom space, or auditorium. The extent to which technology is provided to assist with the presentation may vary considerably. When technology is available consider all alternatives, such as the use of an iPad, a wireless laptop computer, or an audience response system (i.e., clickers). It is possible, however, that the task of explaining how to navigate the library's web pages may have to be done without the use of a computer. Never assume what equipment and access is available. Always check ahead and plan accordingly. Allow enough time to make adjustments or changes to the choice of medium. Always have backup plans in case disaster strikes or a glitch (such as loss of Internet access or flash drive malfunction) should arise. Liaisons must be mobile, plan ahead, and know all of the presentation options.

Regardless of the chosen medium, each orientation meeting will need to cover some basic topics. There are a number of ideas that can be incorporated into these presentations. Some of these may include the library mission and a summary of the numerous ways the library can assist faculty and staff. Also include in the presentation a list of resources, including books, newspapers, magazines, CDs, e-books, database collections, thesis and research papers, a library map, and key library web pages. Illustrate how to find im-portant library information online. Everyone will also need to understand how to log in to access information, database materials, and e-books from remote loca-tions. Rules regarding borrowing, material and equipment checkout, copy-right, reserving rooms and computer labs, and interlibrary loans are all basic presentation topics. Additionally, the areas of information literacy (IL) assis-tance and arranging IL classes should be mentioned.

Keep in mind that depending on the audience, interest levels will vary on these basic topics and the presentation should be tailored accordingly. No orientation will cover every topic. In fact, sometimes it helps to discuss with other library staff or faculty ahead of time what is the most important information and what should be prioritized. Include information of interest to specific departments if possible. Show how the library can assist their department in meeting their specific information needs. For example, if the meeting is for science faculty members, introduce any new subscrip-tions to databases that would benefit their classes. If there is a special library on campus (such as a music library), have a representative attend to give highlights of the collection. If the orientation is for administrative support staff, mention any delivery service that brings library materials directly to the department. Faculty as well as administrators may be interested in con-ference rooms located in the library or equipment available for conference room presentations. These are all examples of illustrating how the library can help the various orientation attendees achieve their own specific goals. This will personalize the relationship between the library staff and the rest of the academic community and enhance the value of the library and its services. Ideally, all orientation attendees should be invited to tour the library in per-son to familiarize themselves with the location of materials, computer labs, and other resources. Library tours can follow the orientation meeting or be offered at another time. It would be a plus for a library liaison to tour with faculty and staff as this further promotes the growing relationship that is so critical to success. Consider appointments for tours as well as select times for an open house. A virtual tour of the library could also be important. A tour of this kind could be accomplished in any number of creative ways, which include video production and screencasts. (Details on creating these types of tutorials are covered in chapter 4.)

Librarians often find orientation meetings limited to thirty minutes. In these cases there is often internal debate on topics and depth of coverage. Based on the audience, information relayed should be prioritized, with less critical information included as time allows. A presenter should use advance practice to correct timing of these presentation areas. Staying within a pre-assigned time allowance will allow for all critical information areas to be covered, even when time is short. Regardless of the amount of time, remember this is both a learning experience and a marketing pitch.[1] You need to hook the audience by getting them to understand the important role of the library and liaisons and how they can be utilized to meet their needs. Due to time constraints it may be necessary to "tease" their interest in library holdings and services. Inform them in concrete ways how the library can further their research projects and assist with class assignments. For example, share specific success stories using the names of their colleagues. Once they reach out to the liaison, the opportunity to promote more of the library resources and services is available. Often the orientation meeting is the first impression. Make it good! Leave them wanting to come back for more.

The orientation should include an introduction of the library staff. If possible, have the library staff attend or stop in during the orientation meeting to personally greet the attendees. (Sometimes library staff can participate as attendees in other nonlibrary elements of orientation as well.) Remember, when the goal is building relationships, you should not underestimate the value here of this participation. It is hoped that through the orientation process general faculty and other attendees will have a chance to link a face to their assigned liaison's name. If possible, these librarians can introduce themselves, explain their areas of subject expertise, and summarize their library duties. For example, if only select liaisons actually teach information literacy classes or if one librarian handles interlibrary loans, it is important for faculty to know who these individuals are and how to contact them. If a librarian is unable to attend, be sure to show a picture or profile video link (if available) and introduce his or her subject areas of focus. All library staff pictures, names, and contact information should be included in the PowerPoint presentation and on handouts. Make it easy to connect in whatever manner the nonlibrary staff or faculty member is most comfortable.

Using handouts with important information is also recommended during the orientation meeting. Even with a PowerPoint or Internet presentation, handouts are something attendees can take with them and refer back to at a later time. Included in the handout package could be a list of critical links, existing or new library resources, useful forms (such as materials or an interlibrary loan request), and library liaisons with contact information.[2] (Many library forms are electronic so include the appropriate links.) A list of databases with summaries and full-text availability would also be useful, including guidelines on accessing electronic information from both library and remote locations. You might also include general library policies, library hours, rules for checking out or reserving materials, how to access available equipment, and any other pertinent library information. Guidelines for booking an information literacy class, including lead time and assignment requirements, could be in the handouts as well. While these worksheets should be concise, including a hard copy of all areas covered in the presentation as well as important information for which time constraints may restrict in-depth coverage is a good idea.

Finally, an ideal orientation meeting would include food and be fun! While orientation presentations are often lost in day-long meetings, adding a twist would make it memorable. Including breakfast or lunch can not only extend interaction time with personnel but also increase attendance. What better way to get all the faculty and staff to the meeting? Make it a tradition! This is also a great way for library liaisons to interact with faculty and staff in a relaxed social atmosphere. Providing goodie bags or even a raffle giveaway at the end of the presentation will guarantee a positive experience.[3] It will also promote annual attendance at an event that many existing faculty members would rather skip. Make the orientation fun!

Presentation Essentials Checklist

□ Medium
□ Audience assessment
□ Topics to cover
□ Library tour

□ Introduction of staff
□ Handouts
□ Food and fun

Faculty Orientations

Faculty orientations are often broken down into two different meetings—new faculty and returning faculty. Each group will have different needs and expectations for the orientation meeting. While some aspects of the presentations will be the same, new faculty will need an emphasis on the basic library information, collections, and services. Returning faculty will be more interested in additions and changes to the library resources and activities.

For new faculty members, coverage of information such as the library's location, material checkout, general library holdings, library services, document delivery, reserves (electronic, book, and media), navigating the library website, and available equipment is important. New faculty members also need to know how to request their own library cards as well as cards for graduate assistants and family members if these borrowing privileges are allowed. The importance of information literacy and the school's accreditation should be discussed as it relates to library services. Also, provide the URL for any specific faculty pages or helpful web pages that target faculty needs. If the presentation has a live connection to the library website, take attendees through the faculty pages and highlight the main areas of information. New faculty should also be made aware of special rooms for classroom instruction or faculty collaboration that the library provides. A general collection overview should be given to these new hires. If possible, lead these professors through the library website online and explain how to access a repository of faculty works and dissertations.

For returning faculty members, remember to emphasize what is new and different in the library from the previous school year. This would include additions to the collection, databases, multimedia, library guides, study spaces, equipment, computer labs, and any changes to library services impacting faculty. Once again, tailoring library resources specifically to departments is a plus. Changes to the library website for the returning faculty members should be mentioned and illustrated online if possible. Noting website alterations is important so returning faculty do not become frustrated in locating information that may have been moved. Be selective with information for returning professors. Keep them engaged, not bored!

It is important that all new materials (books and multimedia) and database holdings are reviewed in both new and returning faculty orientation meetings. Point out library collection improvements through print and database additions. Also take a moment to mention that library liaisons are available to assist with these new information sources if a professor has to plan a class project or lecture presentation. Be positive about the collection and let faculty know the library is there to meet their needs and those of their students.

At most institutions faculty research is important to both professors and their departments. As a requirement of the position, especially when it involves tenured faculty, research projects are an area where librarians can help. Point out any special assistance the library or the liaisons provide with research projects and remind faculty that interlibrary loan (ILL) is available to access materials not within the collection. Review the ILL policy, including the ordering and delivery of materials requested. If faculty members have extended borrowing privileges, intrauniversity borrowing privileges, or checkout recall it is good to mention these perks. Also of value to faculty members who are interested in publishing are information about and links to academic journal rankings, acceptance rates, and citation usage information. Citation assistance such as RefWorks and citation guides may also be helpful to faculty members doing research. If possible, provide real examples of how the library has assisted with faculty projects in the past. This will help establish trust in the reliability of library services.

Copyright is another important area to touch on in all of the faculty orientations. While there may not be enough time to go into depth on this topic, faculty should be reminded of basic copyright policies and how these may affect their use of published information. An overview of the fair use of materials with regard to purpose, nature, amount, and financial impact should be considered. Special laws for online teaching (TEACH Act) is copyright information faculty need to know.[4] Provide the name and contact information of the library's copyright specialist. If the library or university website offers copyright assistance through website links (laws, compliance statement, organizations, and copyright records) or online tutorials, it also could be pointed out to faculty members.

Special faculty support can be delivered in different ways, and it can make faculty's use of library holdings and services easier. This support may be delivered through research guides, faculty information pages, class pages, plagiarism tools, or media equipment. The fact that the library has a computer lab or multimedia viewing room may be exactly what the professor needs to know. Many libraries may have a lab for audio and video creation and Macintosh computers with special design software. Mention any additional means for faculty updates on library announcements throughout the year by newsletters, electronic discussion list feeds, or blogs. Faculty support may also come in the form of adding library liaison contact information, electronic reserves, subject guides, videos, and other pertinent information resources to classroom software (such as Blackboard or Moodle). Embedded librarians can provide these resource lists and other help to the students. Let the professors know this assistance is available and to contact their liaison for additional information.

Information literacy is a large component of libraries and liaison work at colleges and universities. Depending on institutional support, some IL services are conducted only at the request of the faculty and others are an integrated part of the curriculum. Proactive information literacy is often the result of accreditation requirements. During orientation meetings, the library's role and the services it can provide (including teaching IL classes) should be discussed. Guidelines for working with liaisons or IL instructors, scheduling classes, and understanding how IL is delivered (such as a web conferencing option) should also be reviewed. Again, the emphasis should be upon utilizing the liaison relationship.

Faculty need to know about the library's acquisitions process in their orientation meeting. How do they order new materials? How can a liaison assist in this selection? The budget allocation may be based on the number of students for a major, the number of courses offered, prior rates of spending, cost of materials, number of faculty, and usage statistics.[5] Also, the criteria used to prioritize requests need to be explained. Sometimes the final decision lies in the hands of the department while other times the library will make the final choice when ordering new materials. Faculty should be encouraged to contribute suggestions for expanding the holdings. Mention that liaisons can facilitate suggestions with sources such as Choice Reviews Online (which has its own Facebook page) or Yankee Book Peddler's Global Online Bibliographic Information (GOBI) alert system if offered by the library. If the library has materials the faculty need and use it benefits everyone, especially students.

Library collection strengths and weaknesses should not be ignored during orientation talks.[6] Not all libraries have everything, and faculty members should be tailoring projects to coordinate with library resources. Point out the positives in the holdings and services. However, also indicate areas that need improvement or where budget restrictions have limited resources. Faculty need to know what they realistically have at their disposal with regard to research materials, services, equipment, and spaces. With this information they can more effectively plan their courses.

During faculty library tours, emphasize areas of the library these personnel may utilize, such as a computer lab for classes or a faculty-only media space. If a physical tour is not possible during the orientation, always invite them to the library. During virtual tours of the library website, review how to search for materials, access database articles, locate a faculty resource page, request materials, put materials on reserve, and contact their liaison. Both physical and virtual tours should be a part of all faculty orientations. Even returning faculty can learn something new about the library.

Finally, tell faculty members they are critical to the library's success. They need to know how important they are from the library's perspective, and they should hear this in the orientation meeting. These professors will be writing the assignments for which students utilize library resources and will be scheduling IL classes. They will be contacting liaisons for assistance with integrating information literacy and creating well-written assignments. These instructors will also be working with liaisons to locate or purchase collection materials to support their class instruction. Professors pitching a new course will need liaisons to assist with information regarding available resources to support the proposals. All these activities involve library assistance. Faculty members need librarians, but *librarians* need *faculty*. These professors are in many ways the most important segment of the library's "customer base." Just as Ken Blanchard and Sheldon Bowles suggest in their classic book on customer service, *Raving Fans*, make these faculty members raving library fans![7]

When the orientation meeting is completed, it is important to do two final steps—evaluation and follow-up. Feedback from attendees can provide important insight into the effectiveness of the orientation meeting. Use short evaluation surveys (either on paper at the end of the meeting or by e-mail at a later time) that include questions about what information was most useful, which topics of interest were not covered, and recommendations for future meetings. Follow up after the orientation meeting with an e-mail to all faculty members that thanks the attendees and includes attachments of handouts, critical information, and links professors can save in electronic form. This also provides the essential information to faculty who may have missed the orientation gathering. Evaluation and follow-up should not be skipped. Next year the orientation will be even better!

> ### Faculty Orientation Meeting Topic Checklist
>
> ☐ Collection overview
> ☐ Research support/materials
> ☐ New materials/databases
> ☐ Library services and support
> ☐ Copyright information
> ☐ Information literacy assistance
> ☐ Library strengths and weaknesses
> ☐ Physical and virtual tour
> ☐ Marketing pitch—importance of faculty

Administrative Staff Orientations

While connecting to faculty members is critical to the success of the library, often forgotten is an orientation meeting for the college's or university's administration and support staff. A key difference in planning this orientation meeting compared to one for faculty members is that these personnel will typically be coming to the library with one specific goal or project in mind.[8] The library may be just the place for information critical to projects and proposals. For example, information on demographics, marketing trends, educational trends, or academic studies found at the library may prove valuable to administrators, or a library conference room may be the perfect setting for a support staff meeting. Both groups need to know what the library can offer and understand the basic steps for utilizing the library to meet their needs.

The liaison should consider two avenues for reaching the educational support staff. First, returning employees can be treated in a similar manner as returning faculty members. This orientation meeting can be tailored to point out changes and modifications to library resources and services. A second avenue is to pursue the appropriate new employees at the college or university. Working with the human resources department will allow liaisons to tailor library information, a library tour, or even a presentation to the new hires who will utilize the library resources. It is a good idea for liaisons to employ the assistance of their library director when pursuing new hires through the human resources department.

In addition to information, the library can provide, as mentioned, meeting rooms, media equipment, and specialized software to support administration and other staff members. Included in the orientation should be a list of all the available materials and services that may be useful to these personnel. This may include things such as video players or recorders, electronic readers, display tables, and laptop computers. Also include any meeting room spaces as well as video/audio labs that may be useful. Staff members may find special graphics, website, and design software useful, and if technology support is available, that is a plus.

Placing materials on reserve is a common request among faculty. Guidelines for accomplishing this along with any limitations on number of items or length of time should also be explained. A review of any necessary reserve forms (either on paper or online) and information on delivery of materials (if available) should be reviewed. Staff members should feel comfortable reserving materials for their departments.

The involvement of faculty members in the collection development process may extend to their support staff as well. A brief overview of the acquisitions process could be helpful for these personnel. Included should be the process for new material requests and the effect of funding on such requests. For example, if there are funds set aside for purchases throughout the year, what are the limitations? How far in advance must a request be made to ensure it can be added to the collection for use in a class? What are key budgetary dates for future purchases that may arise? If support staff has an awareness of the acquisitions process, they can better assist faculty members if requested.

The orientation meeting should also inform staff members as to the process of checking out resources such as a book, magazine, or DVD. Review library policies that affect their use and be sure to include steps for getting a library card for the new employees. What special privileges are extended to these staff members? Are items used for class purposes allowed to be checked out for longer periods of time? Also, encourage staff members to use the library to check out books to read for personal enjoyment. Once again, the overarching goal is about establishing relationships and the greater amount of contact, even if for personal use, benefits everyone in the long run.

Often libraries are the source for copy machines for staff members. Review the number and location of copy machines as well as their capabilities. For example, are two-sided copies and stapling options available? Does the machine group papers automatically? Does the library have a color copier available? The logistics of paying for copies by these staff members should also be reviewed. For example, does the department have an electronic card for making copies outside of their immediate office? Are copies free or charged back to the department?

Reserving rooms and media equipment is something all support staff will do at some point during the school year. Many libraries now allow self-booking of rooms. In addition to indicating what rooms are available, their sizes and description, also review the policy for room reservation. How far in advance can a room be reserved? Are there any limitations? What spaces are available for class sessions and is there computer access? If there is a media room that can be reserved, bring this to the attention of the staff. Also note any rooms that may be suitable for a formal business meeting held by administrators. As in the faculty orientation meeting, provide a list of equipment available for staff members along with checkout guidelines and limitations, such as equipment (for example, audio/video equipment or in-house DVD players) that must be used only in the library.

All administration and staff should know how to use the library website. If possible, an online demonstration highlighting key areas of the website should be planned. The orientation meeting should deliver a review of how to search the catalog as well as sample searches in some of the library's subscribed databases. If any subject guides are available, point those out as well. These could assist staff members in locating the information they need. Make a special note if there is a library guide specific to assisting faculty and staff with basic library operations and services. Always encourage them to contact their department's library liaison for assistance and provide liaison contact information both in print and online.

Finally, encourage feedback during your orientation meeting. Ask participants about their potential projects and requests to see how the library may assist. Communication is essential to matching library support with staff needs. Consider a brief written evaluation at the end of the meeting to determine not only how informative the meeting was but also what topics and issues not covered may be of help. Often people are more comfortable writing a suggestion than voicing one. Always be open and receptive to staff and administrative needs. Once again, establish the personal connection as a library liaison so that these special personnel will be comfortable with asking for help.

Administration/Support Staff Orientation Topic Checklist

☐ Available materials   ☐ Copy machines

☐ Reserves   ☐ Reserving media and materials

☐ Acquisitions process   ☐ Conference rooms or classrooms

☐ Retrieving resources   ☐ Database review

Conclusion

As preparation for orientation meetings begins, keep in mind that these gatherings are more than a presentation to the academic community. They are a piece of a relationship puzzle—liaisons connecting with other faculty and staff. As a library liaison, building trust with faculty and other academic personnel allows communication to flow from library to academic departments. If successful, this relationship not only positively affects the individual student in the classroom but also contributes to the overall goals of the academic community.

NOTES

1. Caitlin Tillman, "Library Orientation for Professors: Give a Pitch, Not a Tour," *College and Research Library News* 69, no. 8 (2008): 470.

2. Leslie Hurst, "The Special Library on Campus: A Model for Library Orientations Aimed at Academic Administration, Faculty, and Support Staff," *Journal of Academic Librarianship* 29, no. 4 (2003): 238.

3. Tillman, "Library Orientation," 471.

4. Kenneth Crews, "New Copyright Law for Distance Education: The Meaning and Importance of the TEACH Act," *American Library Association*, 2002, www.ala.org/Template.cfm?Section=Distance_Education_and_the_TEACH_Act&Template=/ContentManagement/ContentDisplay.cfm&ContentID=25939.

5. Kitti Canepi, "Fund Allocation Formula Analysis: Determining Elements for Best Practices in Libraries," *Library Collections, Acquisitions, and Technical Services* 31, no. 1 (2007): 19–20, http://opensiuc.lib.siu.edu/cgi/viewcontent.cgi?article=1021&context=morris_articles.

6. Tillman, "Library Orientation," 471.

7. Kenneth Blanchard and Sheldon Bowles, *Raving Fans: A Revolutionary Approach to Customer Service* (New York: William Morrow, 1993).

8. Hurst, "Special Library," 235.

Subject Expertise

One major component to a liaison's success is acquiring subject knowledge. The academic liaison must have an understanding of specific topics in order to assist faculty. Without an understanding of what faculty members are teaching, connecting specific library resources to their needs is impossible. Having this knowledge prior to consideration for hire at an academic center is useful and even preferred by some institutions. However, studies have shown it is not always required in advance, with skills in communication, teaching, and outreach gaining in importance.[1] Working with fellow librarians and faculty as well as actively learning about a subject once assigned to an area are critical attributes for the liaison.[2]

Many academic communities are divided by subject, such as humanities, business, fine arts, natural sciences, health sciences, and social sciences, to name just a few. Community colleges may have even more specialized areas related to specific jobs in such fields as automotive, construction, culinary arts, dental hygiene, real estate, or banking. These colleges may also offer courses in dance, art, home and garden, and sports. In varying academic environments, the library liaison will typically be assigned to one or more of these subject areas and be expected to interact with the instructors teaching these classes. Liaisons must be knowledgeable about these disciplines in order to communicate with faculty conceptually and be able to assist them with information literacy instruction, library guides, research projects, and other methods of support. Initially, becoming a subject expert may appear daunting, but there are a number of sources and support groups to utilize. Liaisons new to the job should not be overwhelmed by what lies ahead! Becoming a subject expert takes time and is a never-ending task. There will always be new theories, studies, and writings to explore. Learning is a lifelong process, and becoming a subject specialist will take patience and initiative. However, the sources provided in this chapter provide a good starting point for liaisons to acquire subject knowledge.

Faculty Resources

To be effective, academic library liaisons must acquire the necessary understanding of a specialized subject. While liaison positions differ, many of these librarians become experts in one or more areas. Some of these librarians will already have a foundation of information to build on from previous experiences or educational backgrounds. How extensive those building blocks of information are will affect how much work must be done to be knowledgeable in a particular topic. Regardless of the level of expertise, there is always more to learn, and staying current on issues will allow the liaison to connect to the assignments and research projects that professors may be designing for students.

Faculty members and the classes they teach are an excellent resource for subject knowledge. These instructors are professionals in their field and have studied extensively to achieve their status. Librarians can utilize them to expand their personal understanding. Attending faculty lectures is one method of gaining knowledge through this association. In addition, liaisons can solicit general faculty feedback and advice, investigate faculty research projects, and review classroom assignments.

Soliciting faculty feedback on a subject specialty can occur at any time. These exchanges can be casual or formally solicited by the library liaison. The variety of methods and importance of establishing a good relationship with faculty members are covered extensively in chapter 3. The key is first establishing a relationship. Once the relationship is well established, the liaison will learn more from the faculty member with regard to his or her specialty. Topical questions can be addressed individually or tied to other liaison duties. For instance, liaisons can explore specific subject areas when preparing for an information literacy class since these classes should relate to the subject studied or a specific assignment for the students. Other opportunities for conversation with faculty can be connected to assisting with information literacy in creating classroom assignments, updating library guides, creating embedded classroom resources, or during collection development communications. Use these opportunities for faculty input and explanation of their courses. These interactions are opportunities for learning.

Investigating faculty research projects and reading publications also enlighten librarians. Besides being informative, these projects can be interesting. For example, 2012 studies at Clemson University's Department of Psychology include topics such as "Fitness and the Workplace," "Cyber Bully-ing," and "Human-Centered Computing."[3] The University of Mississippi uploads online summaries of faculty book publications.[4] The Harvard Law School offers online search for their faculty journal publications.[5] Since faculty tenure involves such publications, there are numerous opportunities for library liaisons to benefit and expand their subject knowledge both within their own academic center as well as in universities throughout the country.

Finally, obtaining a class syllabus to review classroom assignments is extremely helpful to liaisons because it gives insight into assignments, student learning, and current topics. If the class syllabus is not readily available, liaisons should make an effort to obtain a hard copy or Internet access to the material. This is not always an easy task. Often, if librarians are not embedded into a class, online access is restricted. They must seek out this information. There may be a policy-based institutional avenue for gaining access or the need to contact a department chair or an individual faculty member as part of this process. Once obtained, review the syllabus for valuable information. The liaison can now concentrate on specialized areas of subject matter to assist directly with resource and research support. What are the students reading? Researching? Exploring? Liaisons should explore these same concepts if they are unfamiliar with them or their knowledge base is thin. This process will also give liaisons a chance to see where they can assist with the class in the form of information literacy, library guides, research resources, and collection development. (More on classroom collaboration between the librarian and professor is covered in chapter 5.) Knowing what areas to focus on within the subject area before the actual classes begin is a huge asset to the liaison.

Liaisons should use faculty resources to their advantage. Casual or work-related interaction with instructors provides opportunities for learning. Additionally, investigation into faculty books, journal articles, and other publications provides insight into the subject as well as their personal interests. Finally, obtaining the all-important classroom syllabus to directly connect to what is being taught in the classroom is of great value to the liaison. Through the syllabus the liaison can focus personal subject learning efforts on areas that will have the greatest impact on the students. The liaison is even more effective armed with knowledge from faculty resources.

Faculty Resources Checklist

- ☐ Soliciting faculty feedback on subject
- ☐ Faculty research and publications
- ☐ Classroom assignments

Education

Subject expertise can also be achieved through liaison education. Regardless of a liaison's level of expertise, learning continues throughout a career and liaisons should set aside time to broaden their knowledge base. The wealth of subject knowledge should always be expanding. To accomplish this, liaisons will find new information through three educational avenues—independent study, interacting with others, and formal training.

Independent study is a simple, inexpensive way for liaison librarians to gain additional knowledge of their assigned subject areas. While there are any number of ways to approach independent study, one method is to break down the areas of learning into small sections. Start with writing down the name of the college for the subject area assigned. Underneath this header, note the subtopics or individual departments. For example, under a College of Business may be departments such as paralegal studies, accounting, international business, and marketing. Each of these departments will have a number of core courses and electives. Begin the search for knowledge initially in courses that are currently taught (or scheduled for the upcoming term) and in courses where there will be liaison interaction. Time will be valuable as liaisons learn on the job, so start with areas of information that will be immediately applied. (It is also helpful at this point to note which faculty members are assigned instructors of these classes since communication is soon to come.) Write down the courses to target. Search for information on courses not being currently taught for a later time—either the next term or over the summer break.

Once the current, selected courses are determined, become familiar with the overall subject. A general overview of the topic and understanding of concepts it covers may be achieved through a general reference resource. For example, if the College of Business marketing department offers a business-to-business course or a consumer behavior course, learn how the department defines the course within its curriculum. What concepts do business-to-business or consumer behavior actually cover at the academic institution? Once an overview is determined, move on to the course description and begin doing research on the topic. Approach the learning process as if writing a research paper. Do some investigative work. If necessary, return to the reference sources and make notes. Next, acquire the textbook for the course and begin reading. While time may limit a cover-to-cover read, do understand what the course is about and how it is divided. Begin thinking about library resources and what may be available to supplement the instruction. Are there books, journals, databases, or audio or video resources that may be relevant?

After a general subject study and textbook review are completed, begin to search through these sources. The first area to begin with could be a database review. Explore all relevant databases for information about the subject. (In

The University of Florida Health Science Center Libraries' Suggested Learning Methods for Subject Expertise

Vendor and database training:

- Biotechnology presentations
- Medical Library Association continuing education
- Departmental seminars
- Reading dissertations

SOURCE: Michele Tennant, Linda Butson, et al., "Customizing for Clients: Developing a Library Liaison Program from Need to Plan," *Bulletin of the Medical Library Association* 89, no. 1 (2001): 14.

the business example used, the Business & Company Resource Center would be a relevant database resource.) Spend time reading or scanning articles to acquire even more topical information. Discern any related audio or video recordings that may be relevant to the course. (It would be good to make note of materials that the professor may find helpful in instruction during this part of the process.) Next, review books and in-house magazines or journals in the library collection focused on the subject area. Make note of these resources and the type of information they contain. Again, this will be useful material for other liaison duties such as teaching information literacy or creating library guides or pathfinders. Another source of good information often ignored is student dissertations where a topic is already researched and thoroughly covered.

This is an excellent way to learn about subject specialties in a short amount of time. Make use of existent work and research! While other approaches to independent study may differ, reference materials, books, articles, video and audio recordings, and dissertations are still the core of initial learning. Designate time each week for study and education. Monthly or quarterly goals (such as reading five new articles and two new books in a semester) will keep subject learning on track and a priority in the busy liaison work schedule. Remember, the more information a liaison can learn, the more valuable he or she is to the faculty and students he or she serves. As the knowledge base grows, the liaison will be more confident and capable in his or her role. While not ideal as the only learning method, through independent study this can be achieved.

Subject Area Breakdown, College of Business

Paralegal studies. Introduction to Legal Profession, Real Estate Law, Legal Writing

Accounting. Economics 1 and 2, Business Finance, Principles of Management

International business. International Financial Management, International Business, Export Marketing, Global Logistics

Marketing. Fundamentals of Marketing, Retailing, Buyer Behavior

The second avenue for acquiring knowledge is by interacting with others. Valuable information can be exchanged between individuals if communication is established. Do not be afraid to seek out information! A twelve-year study by Ann Baker, Patricia Jensen, and David Kolb illustrated that learning through conversation is real and evolves over time.[6] In the beginning of the relationship, only the recipient benefits from a more knowledgeable individual, but eventually their conversation becomes an exchange of ideas.[7] Liaisons can learn subject information from others, and eventually share ideas as well. Some key person-to-person contacts come from sources such as fellow librarians, lecturers, journal clubs, blogs, and electronic discussion lists.

One of the best sources of subject knowledge is fellow librarians. A formal mentorship program facilitates this interaction. However, depending on the library, a formal mentorship program may or may not be available. In an organization where a mentorship program is in place, other library liaisons can provide vital information on subject areas and available resources. Kansas State University Library has had an academic librarian mentorship program in place for over twenty years to improve staff skills.[8] An excellent summary of their program was published in 2009. Keys to their program success include having volunteer (rather than mandating) mentors, individual as well as group mentorship activities, goal setting, and program assessment.[9] A similar mentorship program assists librarians at the University of Florida's George A. Smathers Library, which implemented a structured, six-year mentorship model in 2010.[10] These models illustrate that mentorship works. If mentorship is not a formal component of library training, aligning with one or more fellow librarians will enhance success. Liaisons should ask questions and seek advice from other librarians who can provide excellent knowledge on subject areas. The informal mentors can not only direct the learning liaison to relevant subject resources but also make suggestions in the areas of information discussion lists, conferences, associations, and workshops.

Interaction with others can also take place by attending subject-related events. These could include faculty lectures, guest lectures, and general class attendance. Liaisons not only learn more about a subject specialty, but they also show support for a faculty member when attending a formal lecture. As noted previously, sitting in on an actual class is an excellent way to learn more from professors themselves. Try to find time to attend a class. (Build that liaison-faculty bond at the same time!) If the academic community is hosting a noteworthy speaker in the field, add it to the schedule. Even if the material covered is something familiar, it will provide a great topic to discuss with faculty the next day. Consider taking notes on these occasions to keep focused and to have a record of ideas discussed. Utilize the subject experts who are themselves in the academic communities!

Another method of interacting with others to obtain subject knowledge is through online journal clubs, blogs, and discussion lists. These online venues bring together professionals who comment on specific topics or publications relating to one field. These groups provide up-to-date information through discussions that can add to the subject liaison's knowledge. Many online journal clubs are related to the scientific or medical fields. For example, the American College of Physicians has an online journal club that focuses on relevant, peer-rated journal articles.[11] This club detects the most relevant medical disorder articles, summarizes them, and discusses their content.[12] This is a perfect time-saver for learning subject liaisons! Online blogs are another source of subject-specific information posted by professionals in the field. Again, in the area of science, the American Association for the Advancement of Science offers a blog on current topics and opinions.[13] Another example is the Social Psychology Network, which maintains links to over 100 psychology blogs, podcasts, and RSS feeds at www.socialpsychology.org/blogs.htm.[14] Subscribing to association discussion lists is another way to expand knowledge through online interaction. For instance, the American Sociological Association offers both announcement and discussion list feeds to members.[15] (An associate membership is only $47 per year.) Library liaisons should investigate subject associations for the availability of online information through all of these online club, blog, and discussion list sources. Since time is often limited, liaisons should pick one or two sources that provide good information for each subject area.

The third avenue for acquiring information on subject specialties is through formal training methods. The setting of formal sessions and gatherings is an excellent environment in which to expand subject knowledge. For many, a specific date and supported learning experience are necessary for learning. These formal training methods may include continuing education classes, conferences, webinars, in-service training, library training programs, and library retreats. These educational experiences can be an interesting time-out from regular work duties.

The first formal method, continuing education, may include instructional classes offered by a nearby college or university or through online distance education. What better way to increase subject knowledge than to take a class?

Free classes (typically one per semester or quarter) are often a perk of college and university employment. Liaisons should take advantage of this benefit, which is an inexpensive way to increase subject expertise. Community colleges provide courses on a variety of topics that may interest the subject librarian. For instance, specialty classes in the areas of architecture, advertising, business, or graphic arts may fill a knowledge gap for some library liaisons. These are all typical community college programs. Another avenue for continuing education is through education centers and museums outside of the academic communities. Often overlooked, these entities are excellent resources. Some education centers include the National Constitution Center, National Center for Science Education, National Association for Music Education, National Education Association, and EducationUSA. Continuing education can be obtained through museums as well. Museums throughout the country provide interesting subject knowledge resources through programs, events, and exhibitions. A few examples include the Academy of Natural Sciences (Philadelphia, Pennsylvania), Adler Planetarium (Chicago, Illinois), and Museum of Fine Arts (Boston, Massachusetts). The Smithsonian Institution offers a wide variety of resources in all areas as well. Before going, check the museum website for information on showings and special events. Explore the various venues for continuing education through instructional classes, education centers, and museums. Make subject learning fun!

If the extended time commitment of classes or educational visits is not possible, webinars are an efficient way to expand subject area knowledge. Webinars are an excellent resource, and because they are offered online one need only take the time to schedule and watch (or even view recorded webinars). Many of these webinars are low cost or even free. A number of universities post online webinars. While some require association with the school for access, many are free. For example, the University of Wisconsin–Madison offers an IME Video Library with online lectures in over eighty different health subject categories.[16] The University of Northern Iowa has webinars on professional development in education available online as well.[17] A little research will uncover hidden webinar gems for free! In addition to universities, societies and associations provide a variety of webinars as well. American history webinars (free at http://hti.osu.edu/node/349/) were created at Ohio State University in 2010 through a grant from the state's historical society and educational center.[18] Another example comes from the International Association for Food Protection, which offers free webinars on varying topics from food viruses to the consumption safety of leafy green vegetables.[19] Exploring such webinar offerings through universities, associations, and societies is an easy and inexpensive method of learning specific subject information.

Conferences and association gatherings are valuable sources of information as well. Lectures, continuing education courses, and workshops are typically entwined with conferences. Exploration of this avenue of continuing education begins with identifying subject-associated groups and investigating what conferences and meetings they hold. Many groups have national as well as regional gatherings that attract a variety of informative presenters. One example is the American Literature Association, which holds both a conference and a symposium each year offering a wide variety of presentations on the subject of American authors.[20] A liaison to engineering may find valuable information at the International Technology and Engineering Educators Association annual conference.[21] The National Communication Association (NCA) holds an annual national convention, conferences, and regional meetings on a wide variety of topics from intercultural dialogue to ethnography.[22] Past NCA conferences have included business meetings, social interaction, and the theory of persuasion.[23] These topics may be of interest to a communications liaison. Library liaisons will benefit from attending such events to enhance subject knowledge. Funding for this kind of activity will vary considerably across institutions, of course. A multiple-day national conference with registration, travel, per diem, and hotel might cost as much as $1,500–2,000, whereas a local conference might only cost a few hundred dollars or less. Most academic libraries do allocate some funds toward these types of activities, but priorities will be considered in terms of balancing the liaison's professional development–related activities with those of the rest of the staff. If library funding is scarce or if one needs to rely on his or her personal funding, then local opportunities are usually the best option.

In addition to continuing education, webinars, and conferences, the availability of in-service training in the form of workshops or online seminars held for the academic staff may be beneficial. These in-house training sessions can offer opportunities to learn. For example, a culinary arts department may have an on-campus workshop on "The Food of Thailand." If one is able to attend, this would be a great opportunity to learn something new and also get a sense of some of the new information that faculty may soon be incorporating into their classes. The benefits of participating in general faculty in-services cannot be overstated. It gives the liaison a chance to see what policies or pedagogical approaches are being explored and, more important, opens yet another avenue of dialogue with the faculty. Liaisons should take advantage of any off-campus library training programs or retreats that may exist to facilitate subject specialization. Since 1999, the University of Florida Health Science Center Libraries have focused on library staff development and now host an annual retreat and three liaison forums a year.[24] These in-house learning environments are an inexpensive way for liaisons to grow their knowledge base.

Librarians must initiate subject learning to expand their knowledge base. While independent study is one option, it is not the only available avenue. Liaisons should explore in-person interaction with other librarians, faculty, and experts in the field both in-house and outside of the academic center. Educational opportunities also come from classes, subject associations, museums, and webinars. The liaison services are enhanced when subject knowledge is acquired, and it takes a conscious effort to learn a little more every term.

Education Checklist

- ☐ Independent study
- ☐ Learning from others
- ☐ Online clubs, blogs, and discussion groups
- ☐ Continuing education classes
- ☐ Conferences
- ☐ Webinars
- ☐ Retreats and in-service training

Associations and Organizations

Growth and support in the area of subject knowledge can come from external organizations. As mentioned, subject-related associations (such as the American Medical Association or the American Psychology Association) are sources that liaisons should explore. Specific to librarians, the American Library Association (ALA) is a great starting point for information and resources as well. Additionally, state library associations offer continuing education, conferences, forums, blogs, mentoring, and other resources to help liaison librarians. Involvement in associations and organizations will provide the subject librarian with up-to-date information on a variety of topics, including subject specialization.

Some divisions and roundtables of the American Library Association can provide information for the subject librarian. The ALA Learning Round Table focuses on continuing education, materials, and training.[25] Again, the ALA is subdivided into a wide variety of areas that may provide additional relevance specific to a particular subject or discipline. For example, someone serving as a liaison to a discipline which requires a great deal of information about the United States government (e.g., a political science department) might join the Government Documents Round Table (GODORT). The Association of College and Research Libraries (ACRL) offers to members online courses that may relate directly to acquiring subject knowledge. For example, a March 2012 ACRL course titled "Humanities on the Map: Discovering Spatial Humanities" dealt with the use of geography in a variety of subject areas.[26] While not targeted solely to expanding subject knowledge, these groups do offer some resources and information to librarians wanting to acquire knowledge. Librarians should take time to investigate what the American Library Association can offer. There are often opportunities to get involved not just in participating but also in serving on committees and planning events. Imagine planning an event or workshop in conjunction with subject-area faculty or being able to bring this experience back to the faculty on campus!

The American Library Association also delivers a number of discussion list options for academic liaisons. The entire list of feeds is found at http://lists.ala.org/sympa. Liaisons should consider subscribing to some of these academic library information exchanges. On this list, for example, discussion lists for Women and Gender Studies, Science and Technology, Anthropology and Sociology, Slavic and East European, Asian, African and Middle Eastern, and Literature in English are offered by the Association of College and Research Libraries division through its various subsections.[27] The Information Literacy (infolit@ala.org) feed also provides helpful information for liaisons, and continuing education assistance is offered with the Learning Round Table feed (learnrt.ala.org).[28] These discussion list feeds are delivered by e-mail and participants can simply e-mail a response to get involved in ongoing discussion with peers.

Journals are another product of organizations. These specialized publications can provide extensive topical information to the subject librarian. For example, the National Council for Geographic Education produces the

Journal of Geography.[29] *The Journal of American History* is published by the Organization of American Historians at Indiana University.[30] The American Dental Hygienists' Association produces the *Journal of Dental Hygiene* and a more informal magazine titled *Access* providing information for the library liaison at a community college.[31] Many journals today are available through individual organizations' websites. Library liaisons should find reputable journals to explore in the areas they represent. As a starting point, suggested publications can be recommended by faculty members. Faculty may even have issues of a journal accessible only to members that they can share with their favorite liaison! Check to see if the library has a subscription or may be able to include it in the future budget. Organizational journals provide the liaison with up-to-date resources on relevant, associated topics.

Associations and organizations offer great information for library liaisons and should not be ignored. The extent of information they provide through websites, discussion lists, and journals is quite valuable. Again, liaisons should become involved in the American Library Association and any specific organizations connected to their subject areas. All of these resources will help in the growth of subject knowledge and are some of the best ways to learn what the current "hot topic" of a particular field is.

Associations and Organizations Checklist

- ☐ American Library Association
- ☐ Association of College and Research Libraries
- ☐ Discussion lists
- ☐ Subject association journals

Acquisitions

In the library liaison's efforts toward collection development, opportunities for acquiring subject knowledge in a less obvious way also exist. In the search for new or supporting materials for a department of the college or university, liaisons will learn about relevant topics. Subject learning can take place through the collection development process itself. Information can come from suggestions from collections comparisons, book reviews, and vendors.

Determining the current trends in an area often comes from seeing which topics are repeatedly covered when searching for collection items. Hot topics can be determined through a collection comparison analysis often done in the acquisition process. The collection comparison is also good for liaisons to determine what core information the subject consistently covers. (Any unfamiliar subtopics should be explored by the liaison.) Commonalities as well as what may be missing from the collection should be noted through the collection comparisons of relevant academic libraries. While collection development is analyzed in chapter 6, it is worth mentioning its value in the area of subject knowledge.

Book reviews are another good source for generalized information on a topic. As the liaison works to improve and add to the collection, these reviews will be read and analyzed. Through this process liaisons acquire additional information on subject areas. As most librarians know, book reviews are found in *Library Journal*, *Bowker's Books in Print*, *Choice Reviews Online*, Amazon.com, and the *New York Times Sunday Book Review* (available online).[32] Time spent here is of double value as it identifies collection material while making the liaison aware of topics of interest.

Vendors also provide material on subject specialties to encourage their sales. Some provide information on publications if they fit a predetermined profile (such as Library of Congress classification or general subject interest). For example, Ebrary enables liaisons to search by subject and even narrow the topic. One can also be placed on an e-mail list to receive information as new publications appear. Chapter titles as well as sample writings of publications of interest can be read online. Subject knowledge may also be received through video sources when exploring for new collection additions. Films on Demand is an example of a vendor where individual videos or collections of films for libraries can be purchased. (As the name indicates, they are delivered streaming live.) Sorted by subject area, often film clips can be reviewed online before purchase. Free videos such as Ted Talks (www.ted .com) or YouTube postings often provide information on a specific topic a librarian is exploring for collection development. Often vendors provide information on hot items, new releases, and spotlight publications for books, videos, and audio formats. Information from their websites can be used for acquisitions as well as information gathering. Additionally, reading through vendors' magazine advertisements is another way liaisons gain understanding of subject areas.

While not an in-depth method of acquiring subject knowledge, library liaisons do learn through the acquisition process. Collection analysis, book reviews, video clips, press releases, advertisements, and vendor information are among the many ways subject information is imparted. From a broader perspective, one might also consider the fact that the liaison may gain a sense of which of these information sources are the most current or of the greatest value for staying up-to-date.

Acquisitions Checklist

- ☐ Collection comparisons
- ☐ Book reviews
- ☐ Vendor advertising
- ☐ Online video sources

Conclusion

In order to be effective, liaisons must learn about subject specialties. Liaisons must set aside time to explore new material and continue to learn. This enhances not only the relationship with faculty but also the quality of liaison assistance that is delivered. Formal and informal educational avenues are the primary source for acquiring knowledge. Independent study is one method of approaching subject learning. Utilizing mentorship programs, continuing education, workshops, and conferences will enhance learning opportunities. The use of online clubs, blogs, discussion groups, and webinars is also helpful. Subject information is also obtained from associations and organizations, museums, and educational centers. Faculty interaction and publications provide valuable information. Finally, the collection development process gives liaisons a good overview of hot topics. Having a better understanding of a subject area means the liaisons will be more effective in their jobs. Subject specialization affects faculty communications, class assistance, information literacy instruction, embedded librarianship, and collection development. It is, in many ways, the core of the library liaison product, so seek, explore, and learn!

NOTES

1. Jo Henry, "Academic Library Liaison Programs: Four Case Studies," *Library Review* 61, no. 7 (2012): 487–90; Zheng Ye Yang, "University Faculty's Perception of a Library Liaison Program: A Case Study," *Journal of Academic Librarianship* 26, no. 2 (2000): 127; Georgina Hardy and Sheila Corrall, "Revisiting the Subject Librarian: A Study of English, Law, and Chemistry," *Journal of Librarianship and Information Studies* 30, no. 2 (2007): 89.

2. James Thull and Mary Anne Hansen, "Academic Library Liaison Programs in US Libraries: Methods and Benefits," *New Library World* 110, no. 11 (2009): 535.

3. Clemson University, "Clemson Psychology: Faculty Research Projects," *Clemson Psychology*, www.clemson.edu/psych/ugrad/nsf-summer-reu/faculty-research -projects/.

4. University of Mississippi, "Faculty Publications," *Center for the Study of Southern Culture*, http://southernstudies.olemiss.edu/faculty-publications/.

5. Harvard University Law School, "Our Publications," *The President and Fellows of Harvard University*, www.law.harvard.edu/about/publications.html.

6. Ann Baker, Patricia Jensen, and David Kolb, "Conversational Learning: An Experimental Approach to Knowledge Creation," *Experience Based Learning Systems, Inc.*, http://learningfromexperience.com/media/2010/08/the-evolution-of-a -conversational-learning-space.pdf.

7. Ibid.

8. Diana Farmer, Marcia Stockham, and Alice Trussell, "Revitalizing a Mentoring Program for Academic Librarians," *College & Research Libraries* 70, no. 1 (2009), http://krex.k-state.edu/dspace/bitstream/2097/1242/3/Farmer_etal09.pdf.

9. Ibid.

10. Jan Swanbeck and Bonnie Smith, "The Value of Library Mentoring" [PowerPoint slides], www.flalib.org/conference_2011/presentations_handouts/FLA%202011 _Mentoring_Presentation.pdf.

11. "ACP Journal Club: Welcome," *American College of Physicians*, http://acpjc .acponline.org/shared/purpose_and_procedure.htm.

12. Ibid.

13. "Blogs and Communities," *American Association for the Advancement of Science*, http://blogs.sciencemag.org/.

14. Scott Plouse, "Psychology Blogs, Podcasts, and RSS Feeds," *Social Psychology Network*, www.socialpsychology.org/blogs.htm.

15. "ASA Section Listservs," *American Sociological Association*, www.asanet.org/about/ sections/listservs.cfm#Discussion.

16. Board of Regents of the University of Wisconsin System, "SMPH Video Library," *University of Wisconsin School of Medicine and Public Health*, http://videos.med .wisc.edu/categories/.

17. College of Education, "Hot Topics in Education: Professional Development Webinars," *University of Northern Iowa*, www.uni.edu/coe/about/coe-professional-development -webinars.

18. The History Teaching Institute, "Explore History Webinars," *HTI@OSU*, http://hti.osu
.edu/node/349/.

19. "Webinar Archives," *International Association for Food Protection*, www.foodprotec
tion.org/events/webinars/.

20. "An Introduction to the American Literature Association," *American Literature
Association*, www.calstatela.edu/academic/english/ala2/intro.html.

21. "Conference," *International Technology and Engineering Educators Association*,
www.iteea.org/Conference/conferenceguide.htm.

22. "Sponsored Conferences," *National Communication Association*, www.natcom.org/
Secondary.aspx?id=104.

23. "2011 VOICE Conference Program," *National Communication Association*, www
.natcom.org/uploadedFiles/Convention_and_Events/Annual_Convention/97th
_Annual_Convention_2011/2011%20Final%20Program%20Copy.pdf.

24. Michele Tennant et al., "Customizing for Clients: Developing a Library Liaison
Program from Need to Plan," *Bulletin of the Medical Library Association*, 89, no. 1
(2001): 14.

25. "ALA LearnRT," *American Library Association*, www.ala.org/learnrt/.

26. "Humanities on the Map: Discovering Spatial Humanities," *American Library
Association*, www.ala.org/acrl/onlinelearning/elearning/courses/spatialhumanities.

27. "Mailing List Categories," *American Library Association*, http://lists.ala.org/sympa.

28. Ibid.

29. "Publications," *National Council for Geographic Education*, http://ncge.org/
publications.

30. "Issues," *Organization of American Historians*, www.journalofamericanhistory.org/.

31. "Publications," *American Dental Hygienists' Association*, www.adha.org/
publications/index.html.

32. G. Edward Evans and Margaret Saponaro, *Developing Library and Information
Center Collections* (Westport, CT: Greenwood, 2005), 83.

Communication with Faculty

*As a library liaison, prepare to become a master of communication. Commu*nication is the key to establishing faculty relationships, and those relationships lead to success as a liaison. Library liaisons must initiate, establish, and promote their relationships with faculty members in the departments they are assigned to assist. Once there is a connection with faculty, growth and fostering of the relationship are both essential and difficult at times. Everyone has different viewpoints and personalities and will not always agree. Professors will have a different communication style, which means the liaisons must adapt their methods of interaction. However, both faculty and librarians do work toward a common goal—the mission of the academic community. While goals differ between academic communities, ultimately they involve the promotion of education and learning. With persistence the liaison can establish relationships and communication methods with faculty that will have a positive impact in the learning environment. It all begins with the first step—establishing a relationship.

Establishing Relationships

At first glance, establishing a relationship may appear to be easy. How hard is it to say hello? But perhaps it is not as easy as first appears. Both librarians and professors are very busy and typically work in separate buildings. Making contact may not be simple. However, an opportunity to meet some of the faculty members may be available at an orientation meeting or through introductory departmental visits. Adjunct faculty can be a special challenge in this regard since many do not attend these meetings or have convenient office hours. In other situations, it may be that only a list of faculty names and contact information has been provided. Regardless, a library liaison must initiate the first communication with the professors of the assigned subject areas. Consider this initial contact a brief introduction whereby each party can connect a name (and hopefully face) to the role each will play. If at all possible, make contact in person with faculty members initially. If that is not possible, an introduction by phone or e-mail with the invitation to meet later may suffice.

These steps reflect the first two phases of the relationship development model of communication researcher Mark Knapp.[1] They mark the beginning of the connection between librarian and faculty member. Knapp's Relationship Escalation Model identifies five stages of relationship building—initiation, experimenting, intensifying, integrating, and bonding.[2] For liaisons, the first three stages are typically as far as the relationship develops. The initiation stage is short and is the initial, brief contact between a liaison and faculty member.[3] As the interaction grows and the liaison asks questions to learn more about the professor, the relationship expands into what Knapp calls the "experimenting" phase.

In the experimenting phase of the relationship, the opportunity to talk in person finally is achieved. The liaison should spend a few moments in casual conversation before discussing academic needs. It is helpful to find something each faculty member is interested in, and this does not necessarily have to be work related. Learning something new about someone helps build the foundation of the relationship. It is worth noting that while the effort is more purposeful, the elements that go into establishing a good relationship with faculty are no different from those one uses to establish casual friendships and relationships in one's personal life. In any case, identifying areas of interest will be utilized for the second step—the follow-up meeting.

Do not think that contacting a professor just once is enough to gain his or her trust. It is not. Again, as in one's personal life, relationships must be nurtured and developed, and the second step is a follow-up visit. Find a way to expand the relationship with an extended communication or meeting. Ideally, this follow-up would be in a relaxed atmosphere, such as an invitation to have

Faculty Personalization at Rutgers University

Liaisons at Rutgers University collect information on their faculty to set up individual profiles facilitating interaction. The list of information collected includes the following:

- Research and subject interests
- Current research projects
- Courses taught
- Other responsibilities
- Foreign languages
- Academic rank

SOURCE: Connie Wu, Michael Bowman, Judy Gardner, Robert Sewell, and Myoung Chung Wilson, "Fostering Effective Liaison Relationships in the Academic Library," *Rutgers University Libraries*, www.libraries.rutgers.edu/rul/staff/groups/liason_relationship/reports/liason-relationships2.shtml.

coffee or lunch together. While this may not be feasible in all situations, an effort must be made to enhance the connection. It is at this time that the valuable information already learned (the faculty member's topics of interest) is utilized. Use this as an icebreaker in the second meeting before exploring the real needs of the professor. Once the conversation has started, begin to probe areas where a liaison can be of assistance. How can the library help with his or her classes, research, or information literacy needs? What library services has the instructor used in the past? Are there upcoming classroom projects that will require research? Would a class library guide be of assistance? The library liaison will be able to help in some way. The liaison has information and skills that are of value to faculty. This meeting will benefit both parties because it helps determine some areas of need. At this point, the liaison is in line to promote and assist in future communications with faculty.

What exactly does the liaison have that can assist faculty? What are the products and services that will be provided? The answer, of course, involves information, and it is important to think broadly! Information may be delivered through a variety of sources, which include monographs, magazines, databases, e-books, movies and videos, websites, and other relevant contacts on campus. Since the library intersects a variety of departments, librarians can also help to connect faculty and administrators with similar research or project interests. Again, the liaison knows the information, products, and resources best and can match the source to what the faculty member needs in order to teach a class or complete or enhance a project. Assisting with information is just the beginning. The liaison will also work closely with faculty members in the area of collection development to support both current and future classes as well as student research needs. Additionally, the liaison will provide services that include instruction, strategies, and assignment assistance in the area of information literacy. The liaison will also communicate information regarding changes to library policy, services, and collection additions to these educators. Faculty seminars, in-service training sessions, library guides, copyright assistance, online class embedment, and database demonstrations are among the librarian services that may be utilized by the teaching staff and communicated through the liaison. Finally, indicating the availability of library equipment and space (such as class space or faculty labs) may be exactly what the professor needs. The liaison connects instructors to all of these products and services.

Once a relationship is established, the liaison's job is to continue to nurture and promote its growth. These stages of the relationship may eventually lead to what Knapp labels as "intensifying," which indicates when more than an acquaintance develops and a rather less formal interaction between parties takes place.[4] This is the third stage of relationship development. Stay in contact with assigned faculty members throughout the semester. Become familiar with the classes and syllabi and assist when needed. If an information source is relevant, suggest its use to the professor and have it included on the website or within the library subject guide. While supporting these academic instructors, it is important to show interest in their personal growth. Attend faculty lectures and recognize a faculty member who is awarded a grant. Write a congratulatory note about a recent publication. Actually read the publication and ask the professor a few questions about his research in the next communication. Even better, the library liaison can highlight the research project in the library newsletter. Ask if there is a way to assist with research for his or her next project. Everyone likes to be recognized for their hard work, and as a liaison, this is a way to further establish the bond through communication. Liaisons can also further their connections at campus social events and faculty outings. Finally, learn more about the faculty member's hobbies, children, and interests by asking questions. Possibly friend them on Facebook or LinkedIn. People stay connected through social networks more and more, both personal and professionally, and these should not be discounted. The liaison-faculty relationship may last for years, so getting to know the faculty as both instructors and individuals is an asset. Remember, a strong, personal relationship will be the key to success.

While it would be a wonderful world if all faculty members were open and receptive to liaisons and their products and services, this will not always be the case. Librarians will meet resistance in some circumstances. Not all faculty members will be receptive to help and may even perceive the liaison's efforts as intrusive. Research has shown that issues of status, subject knowledge, teaching abilities, and classroom propriety of professors are some of the obstacles librarians will encounter.[5] Liaisons cannot ignore this reality and will not always be successful in forging positive relationships. However, quiet persistence may be the answer for the stubborn professor. Most will come around once they understand the value that can be added and that the liaison is flexible and willing to work around their schedules and needs. Learn faculty interests and understand their needs. Be ready and willing to help at all times. Always be receptive to any contact made and take advantage of opportunities to personalize the relationship. There may be an opportunity in the future to help, so keep the communication open.

Relationship Checklist

- ☐ Initiate contact
- ☐ Follow up
- ☐ Continue outreach
- ☐ Nurture and promote
- ☐ Quietly persist

Communication Methods

Initiating and growing the liaison relationship with faculty is an ongoing process. A variety of methods of communication should be utilized in order to enhance connections and strengthen the relationship between library liaison and faculty member. The method of choice is dependent on faculty preferences, information imparted, and what communication options are available at each university or college. The liaison should have an awareness of what communication formats can be used and which of these is preferred by the professors with whom they interact. Additionally, the type of information imparted will influence the method used. Broader information (such as general library announcements) may use the form of a newsletter. Subject-specific information might be communicated through a subject specialist blog. Personal information, such as resources for a faculty research project, might be best listed in a direct e-mail. All of these forms of communication can be broken down into two categories—real time and asynchronous. Real-time communication is contact between the liaison and instructor in which the exchange of information is instantaneous. Asynchronous communication can be received by either party as time allows. Both methods are typically used by library liaisons.

In-person exchanges are excellent forms of real-time communication. Several university studies have indicated in-person communication is the most effective method of connecting with faculty.[6] In fact, a 2009 study by Forbes Insights indicated face-to-face meetings were preferred because they allowed for relationship building, body language reading, and social bonding.[7] As mentioned in establishing relationships, liaisons should make an effort to talk with faculty through site or office visits, meetings, academic events, or library visits. As a reminder, some instructors do not care for unannounced office visits. Always make an appointment in advance. If there is an opportunity for face-to-face contact with the professional staff, use it!

Meetings are a common source of real-time communication opportunities. A liaison may be asked or required to attend any number of these types of group functions. These gatherings may take the form of faculty meetings, committee meetings, or administrative meetings. Library liaisons should always coordinate attendance at faculty meetings through the respective department heads. Do not be surprised if some department heads are not receptive to a librarian sitting in on these internal meetings. Librarians can be viewed as outsiders to these discussions. However, if the liaison is welcomed, these gatherings allow the librarian to impart library updates and information as well as gather ideas for assisting the department with future projects. In addition to department meetings, liaisons may also be involved in library committee meetings where chosen faculty members represent their subject areas and gather with librarians to discuss the library's impact on educational needs. Once again, this is a valuable opportunity to integrate library services into the classroom. While only the library director or other key library administrators may be involved in curriculum meetings, liaisons may receive valuable information gathered at these sessions to integrate library services early on in new course development. The liaison might work with library administration and critical faculty to establish funding objectives for these new courses or programs. Also important is liaison work with meetings or presentations associated with regional or specialized accreditation, which requires demonstrable integration of library and information literacy–related goals. (Accreditation work is covered extensively in chapter 10.) All of these meetings give library liaisons opportunities to present the library's value in supporting the educational goals as well as the instructors in a face-to-face environment.

While many virtual communication options have been integrated into most academic communities, telephone contact is still highly ranked among faculty. According to one study conducted at a midsized public university rated as having "high research activity" by the Carnegie Foundation for the Advancement of Teaching, Anthony Chow and Becky Croxton discovered that telephone conversation ranks just behind in-person contact and e-mail as the most preferred method of communication for reference-type information.[8] Their study included 551 faculty/staff and suggested that individuals over the age of 55 still *prefer* telephone communication to all other approaches.[9] Telephone communication was also found to be critical in a 2002 Rutgers study that indicates it has also been a long-standing method.[10] While somewhat dated, coupled with the prior study, this indicates a need to not overlook this convenient way to connect with senior faculty.

Finally, a form of instantaneous, personal response can also take place with chat and web conferencing. While not among the top three preferences of faculty, these methods are being used by liaison librarians. Web connections (such as Skype, Unyte, or Windows Live Messenger) allow a visual connection with the use of a simple webcam, which negates the travel time involved with in-person visits. Additionally, the convenience of instant messaging (for example, LibraryH3lp or Plugoo) allows for immediate responses even while other work is being done. Chat is playing an increasing role in liaison-faculty communications because of its ability to give a quick response.[11] These methods will presumably also gain status and value as more and more courses are taught online and it is sometimes impossible for the liaison and faculty member (who may be some distance away) to get together in person. As new software and methods evolve, liaisons must be ready to adapt and use different means of communication.

When choosing the real-time communication method, personal contact with faculty members still ranks as one of the best. If a visit is not possible, phone, chat, or web conferencing are still always options. Checking with each faculty member to determine his or her preferred method is a good idea. Everyone is different, and communication methods are often influenced by age and other demographic factors. However it is done, the personal touch of real-time communication always works well.

Real-Time Communication Checklist

☐ In-person visit
☐ Meetings
☐ Phone
☐ Chat
☐ Web conferencing

Asynchronous communication, or methods that allow each party to respond to inquiries when time allows, can take several forms. These forms include e-mail, discussion lists, newsletters, blogs, social media, mobile apps, and the library website. Liaisons can employ any number of these formats in order to facilitate communication with faculty.

In the area of asynchronous communication, e-mail is still commonly used. However, e-mails should be short and to the point if expected to be read. Readers only spend 15–20 seconds on each e-mail, which indicates that length really does matter. Faculty, already pressed for time, can be especially cursory in reading their e-mail.[12] E-mail is used by every academic community and is also accessible on smartphones. A 2011 study noted that e-mail was the preferred choice, second only to face-to-face contact, of faculty needing assistance.[13] Besides being a flexible communication format in regard to time, e-mail is also preferred by faculty because it provides a written record of information.[14] It is still one of the most common forms of communication between library liaisons and the faculty.

Newsletters are another form of virtual communication. These news briefs are a way to highlight library activities and services. Through newsletters the library can personalize its relationship between faculty and library staff. For example, faculty members can be interviewed about their favorite books or movies. Librarians (including library liaisons) can be highlighted with interesting biographies or stories. Faculty members can be invited to

FIGURE 3.1
Johnson & Wales University, Charlotte Campus Library newsletter

It's Time For...

The Queen City Brew

Volume 5, Issue 5   February 2011

Official Newsletter of Johnson & Wales University's Charlotte Campus Library

Inside this issue:

UPCOMING LIBRARY HOURS

We're coming in on the final stretch of the Winter Term. It's hard to believe! Final projects, papers, and exams are coming up. The Library can help you will all of it.

The Library will have extended hours again during Exam Week. We will stay open until 11 pm on Monday, Tuesday and Wednesday. Tutoring will be available in the back of the Library on those days, as well. If you could use some help getting ready for your exams, check out the schedule (when it becomes available) of what tutoring is available and when.

Once exams are done, the library will have abbreviated hours until the beginning of Spring Term. See our full hours below.

Exam Week	Break
Monday 2/21 8 am – 11 pm	Monday 2/28 8 am – 4 pm
Tuesday 2/22 8 am – 11 pm	Tuesday 3/1 8 am – 4 pm
Wednesday 2/23 8 am – 11 pm	Wednesday 3/2 8 am – 4 pm
Thursday 2/24 8 am – 9 pm	Thursday 3/3 8 am – 4 pm
Friday 2/25 8 am – 4 pm	Friday 3/4 9 am – 4 pm
Saturday 2/26 closed	Saturday 3/5 closed
Sunday 2/27 closed	Sunday 3/6 closed

The Library will resume regular hours on Monday March 7.

We wish you the very best on your exams and final projects!

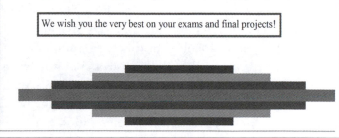

Arizona State University Marketing Strategies

- Attending faculty meetings and orientations
- Sending quarterly newsletter
- Developing liaison program vital information flyers
- Creating one-minute librarian profile videos

SOURCE: Anne Dutton Ewbank, "Education Library 2.0: The Establishment of a Dynamic Multi-Site Liaison Program," *Education Libraries* 32, no. 2 (2009): 5.

create a library guide in the area of their expertise. Also, articles on additions to the collection, digitized projects, exhibitions, and special events can be included. A newsletter example can be found at Johnson & Wales University's Charlotte Campus Library (http://scholarsarchive.jwu.edu/cgi/viewcontent .cgi?article=1004&context=clt_newsletter; see figure 3.1). To keep professors reading, always add items of interest and personalize when possible. Give them a reason to open the newsletter e-mail.

Library blogs are another method to communicate updates on holdings and services. Blogs offer two advantages—a timely upload and easy manipulation.[15] Additionally, faculty can make comments on blog entries, which are an added communication feature. Typically, blogs are put out by the library itself or by subject areas within the library. For a blog example, see figure 3.2. A subject liaison may be assigned to writing or contributing to these blogs. For example, the University of Illinois offers blogs on social sciences, sciences, art, and humanities in addition to other general blogs.[16] Blogs offer a great opportunity to communicate information with faculty. Blog software can be either server installed, such as Subtext or Typo, or hosted remotely, as with Wordpress or Blogger. When blogging, keep the information focused and of interest to the audience. The Ohio University Business Blog, for example, uses Wordpress to give tutorials on finding specific business information in databases or on how to find popcorn consumption in Simply Map.[17] At Ohio State University, thirty library blogs are offered from general news to science and engineering to copyright.[18] In addition to library updates of services and new arrivals, post specialized information that may be of interest to faculty members—especially in subject-specific blogs. For example a 2011 UCLA library blog on art included news on local exhibitions, ARTstor collection

FIGURE 3.2
Georgia State University Library blog

Reprinted with permission.

updates, and subject guide additions.[19] If blogging is a chosen communication method, plan to stay focused and dedicate time to keep posts current. Once started, a blog cannot be neglected or the information is not current and interesting and will soon be left unread. Because blog updates are not typically on a set schedule like monthly or quarterly newsletters, the blogger has the ability to keep information fresh and timely. Blogging may be the perfect solution to enhance faculty communications of library activities.

Social media are yet another medium for virtual communication. Sites such as Facebook and Twitter are often checked daily by users. Faculty can follow or friend the library and receive updates and information this way. The library liaison can make good use of these sites by posting links to stories or information relevant to faculty needs. Given the growing use of such social media sites, they are fast becoming a more important promotional outlet and communication source.

Facebook boasts over 1.15 billion users, with the average user connected to 80 pages and groups.[20] A 2010 multimedia study indicates that 41 percent of the U.S. population has a Facebook profile.[21] This illustrates how social media are playing an increasing role in communication activities. The traditional Facebook page is created by an individual and is divided into four parts—profiles, groups, pages, and events.[22] However, it is recommended that creation of a *page* is the most effective method for a nonpersonal communication such as a message from a subject liaison to followers (the professors).[23] (Profile creation is more for personal use.) Page creation still requires a personal account be in place. To create a page, pick a category (such as organization) and give it an official name before adding a picture and information.[24] An example of naming a page could be the "Henry Library Social Science News." Updates and announcements can be added to the Facebook wall, but there are also areas for discussion, videos, and photographs to keep the page active and informative.[25] To publish, simply upload and then start to provide new information that is relevant to the library followers. Post announcements on collection arrivals or links to relevant articles and send these updates to the faculty fans. One could post a video created on Jing on how to search a relevant database. Keep in mind that to be effective, it will take time to keep the Facebook page current and relevant. Just as when monitoring a blog, Facebook communications need attention. Be sure updates are scheduled at minimum weekly in order to keep this virtual medium current and interest alive.

Twitter has over 230,000,000 active users and is a "great way to build relationships."[26] While Twitter is being used by only 7 percent of the U.S. population over the age of twelve (in contrast to 41 percent using Facebook), it still should be considered as a virtual communication avenue.[27] Many people follow Twitter feeds for information, and library liaison feeds should be considered. (Note that the popular Library Lead Pipe has a Twitter feed.) Twitter accounts allow for individual biographies, but they are limited to 160 characters.[28] Individual tweets, or posts, are limited to 140 characters, but they allow for links to be posted as well as words to lead followers to additional information.[29] Liaisons can make use of URL cutters to shorten URLs (goo.gl or bit.ly) if necessary to fit links into Twitter posts. To post on Twitter, simply fill in the "What's Happening?" box at the top of the Twitter page. For replies, type @username followed by the message. To retweet (resend a message), type RT@username and then copy and paste the message.[30] Like Facebook, Twitter allows communication to be followed by individuals so liaisons can create an account to be followed by faculty and their support staff. Because of its ease of use and ability to broadcast messages quickly, Twitter is another social medium that may be considered when communicating library updates, holdings, and links to faculty followers.

Mobile apps are a growing method of communication. These applications, available through phones and mobile pads, mesh a number of different communication methods. According to a recent study by the Pew Research Center, 39 percent of cell phone users operate on a smartphone platform, and 87 percent of these individuals access e-mail and the Internet through their phone.[31] Given the number of smartphone users, the adaptability of communication methods to connect through the phone is something librarians should also consider when deciding on communication mediums. Smartpads (such as the iPad) are increasingly being used in academia. As an example of the growth of this technology, in 2010 Seton Hill University purchased 1,850 iPads in order to distribute one to each of their students and faculty members.[32] Because iPads have multimedia functions, they can be used as e-book and journal article readers, as podcast players, and as video players. Library liaisons are utilizing them to communicate all types and kinds of information to faculty.[33] They can also serve as an outlet for e-mail communication and wiki exchanges. Many academic libraries are creating their own apps for download or utilizing those provided by vendors of various library-related products and services. Just a few of the companies already on board with apps are SirsiDynix (BookMyne), Gale (AccessMyLibrary), and EBSCOhost.[34] Boopsie Mobile is a company that creates specialized apps for academic libraries which include catalog information, connection to reference librarians, calendars of events, reading lists, social networking feeds, book reserves, and e-book access.[35] These are all examples of how apps as library communication tools are just evolving. As the use of mobile devices spreads, their role as communication devices with faculty will be increasingly important to library liaisons. They will play an increasing role in virtual connections.

A final area of asynchronous communication is through the library website. It is here that liaisons can form their own page with relevant information.

A picture, a profile or informational video, reference sources, and other relevant links can be combined to form a functional communication page with faculty. (How to create an online informational video is covered in chapter 4.) On the website, liaisons can create personal faculty pages with information, research sources, and other tools to assist a specific faculty member. Web pages can also contain important information on copyright as well as offer a convenient online materials request form that faculty members may need. When creating a web page, keep in mind that visitors to this internal page of a website will spend only 45–60 seconds scanning for information, and the majority of time is spent in the middle content area rather than right or left bars.[36] Because of this, be sure to put critical information in the central content area of the website.[37] Additionally, only 42 percent of the users will scroll down interior pages, so make the information above the fold count.[38] Many academic centers have a technology staff to assist with website creation. If this is available, make use of their skills. Creating websites that work is not a simple task. However, creating library websites and web pages is a great method of communication with faculty. Make sure the site contains easy-to-navigate pages of information that faculty members find relevant and helpful.

Liaisons' utilization of virtual-time communications plays a vital role in their ability to communicate effectively with faculty. The choice of medium is dependent on what is well received by faculty and the amount of time a liaison can dedicate to updates. However, with such a wide variety of virtual-time communication options available, there are methods to fit every situation.

Virtual-Time Communication Checklist

☐ E-mail   ☐ Social media sites
☐ Discussion list announcements   ☐ Mobile apps
☐ Newsletters   ☐ Library website
☐ Blogs

Conclusion

Whatever method of communication chosen, it must be easy and convenient for the receiver. It must also meet the information needs of the receiver.

Liaisons can choose from both real-time and virtual-time communications in their efforts to connect with faculty. Through these methods a mix of creativity, efficiency, and news comes together. While virtual options may be quicker and more convenient, real-time connections are more personal and include the important nuances of voice inflection and body expression. Each form of communication has its place in the liaison world, so familiarity with all methods is recommended. Remember—become a master of communication!

NOTES

1. Anu Khanna, "Stage of Relationship Development," *DeAnza College Faculty Files*, Spring 2010, http://facultyfiles.deanza.edu/gems/khannaanu/StagesRelational DevelopmentS.pdf.

2. T. Dean Thomlinson, "An Interpersonal Primer with Implications for Public Relations," in *Public Relations as Relationship Management: A Relational Approach to the Study and Practice of Public Relations*, ed. J. Ledingham and S. Bruning (Mahwah, NJ: Lawrence Erlbaum Associates, 2000), 177–203.

3. Ibid.

4. Khanna, "Stage of Relationship Development."

5. Kristin Anthony, "Reconnecting the Disconnects: Library Outreach to Faculty as Addressed in the Literature," *College & Undergraduate Libraries* 17, no. 1 (February 26, 2010): 83–84.

6. Tom Glenn and Connie Wu, "New Roles and Opportunities for Academic Library Liaisons: A Survey and Recommendations," *Reference Services Review* 31, no. 2 (2003): 122–28; Melissa Kozen-Gaines and Richard Stoddart, "Experiments and Experiences in Liaison Activities: Lessons from New Librarians in Integrating Technology, Face-to-Face, and Follow-Up," *Collection Management* 34, no. 2 (November 2010): 130–42; Anthony Chow and Rebecca Croxton, "Information-Seeking Behavior and Reference Medium Preferences: Differences between Faculty, Staff, and Students," *Reference & User Services Quarterly* 51, no. 3 (2012): 246–62.

7. Jeff Koyen, "Business Meetings—The Case for Face to Face," *Forbes Insights*, http://images.forbes.com/forbesinsights/StudyPDFs/Business_Meetings_FaceToFace.pdf.

8. Chow and Croxton, "Information-Seeking Behavior."

9. Ibid., 255.

10. Glenn and Wu, "New Roles and Opportunities," 124.

11. Chow and Croxton, "Information-Seeking Behavior," 254.

12. G. Simms Jenkins, "Does Email Length Matter?," *iMedia Connection*, www.imediacon nection.com/content/9109.asp.

13. Chow and Croxton, "Information-Seeking Behavior," 255.

14. Ibid., 254.

15. Kozen-Gaines and Stoddart, "Experiments and Experiences in Liaison Activities."

16. University Library, "Library Blogs and Other Social Media," *University of Illinois at Urbana-Champaign*, www.library.illinois.edu/blog/index.html.

17. Chad Boeninger, "Business Blog," *Ohio University Libraries*, 2012, www.library.ohiou.edu/subjects/businessblog/blog.

18. University Libraries, "Blogs," *Ohio State University*, http://library.osu.edu/news/blogs/.

19. Robert Gore, "UCLA Arts Library Art and Art History Blog," *University of California Los Angeles*, http://blogs.library.ucla.edu/art_arthistory/.

20. Facebook, "Newsroom: Key Facts," *Facebook*, http://newsroom.fb.com/content/default.aspx?NewsAreaId=22.

21. Tom Webster, "Twitter Usage in America 2010—The Edison Research/Arbitron Internet and Multimedia Study," *Edison Research*, http://images.publicaster.com/ImageLibrary/account2782/documents/Twitter_Usage_In_America_2010.pdf.

22. Shama H. Kabani, "The Zen of Social Media Marketing" (Dallas, TX: BenBella Books, 2010), 42–43.

23. Ibid., 55.

24. "Introducing New Facebook Pages," *Facebook*, www.facebook.com/pages/learn.php.

25. Ibid.

26. "What Is Twitter?," *Twitter*, https://business.twitter.com/whos-twitter.

27. Webster, "Twitter Usage in America 2010."

28. Kabani, "Zen of Social Media Marketing," 77.

29. "What Is Twitter?," *Twitter*.

30. Kabani, "Zen of Social Media Marketing," 55.

31. Aaron Smith, "Smartphone Adoption and Usage," *Pew Internet & American Life Project*, http://pewinternet.org/Reports/2011/Smartphones.aspx.

32. Mary Ann Gawelek, Mary Spataro, and Phil Komarny, "Mobile Perspective: On iPads Why Mobile?," *Educause Review*, May/June 2012, www.educause.edu/EDUCAUSE+Review/EDUCAUSEReviewMagazineVolume46/iMobilePerspectives OniPadsibrW/226163.

33. Megan Lotts and Stephanie Graves, "Using the iPad for Reference Services—Librarians Go Mobile," *College & Research Libraries News*, http://crln.acrl.org/content/72/4/217.full.

34. Lisa Carlucci Thomas, "The State of Mobile Libraries 2012," *The Digital Shift*, www.thedigitalshift.com/2012/02/mobile/the-state-of-mobile-in-libraries-2012/.

35. "The Complete Mobile Solution for Your Libraries-Features," *Boopsie, Inc.*, www .boopsie.com/library/.

36. Jakob Nielsen and Hoa Loranger, *Prioritizing Web Usability* (Berkeley, CA: New Riders, 2006), 33–35.

37. Ibid., 35.

38. Ibid., 45.

Online Tutorials

Online tutorials can be an effective tool for the library liaison. Information in this format can be accessed by faculty and students from any computer at their convenience. These tutorials can also be very helpful to librarians embedded online who lack the opportunity to meet their students in person. Online tutorials provide information and give students the ability to view it even when a librarian is unavailable or when the library is closed. This any-time access is also part of their appeal and is an effective tool for distance education learners. Topics for such tutorials may include accessing databases, top research sources, citation assistance, study space options, utilizing library guides, or any other pertinent subject that assists in providing assistance to the student. Tutorials for faculty may provide information on topics such as database research, plagiarism, copyright considerations, accessing library resources, or information literacy assistance. For a liaison, transferring knowledge through tutorials can be quite an exciting idea.

Tutorials are actually a subset of a bigger class called learning objects. Lori Mestre, head of the Undergraduate Library at the University of Illinois at Urbana-Champaign, states, "A broad definition of a learning object is that it is a resource, usually digital and web-based, that can be used and reused to support learning."[1] Apart from how they are used by libraries, tutorials could be considered as a method of transferring knowledge or a self-paced train-ing tool. Often tutorials are built in a manner defined as screen capturing or screencasting. Captured keyboard and screen actions are accessed, recorded, edited, and presented so that the viewer of the tutorial understands the steps involved. In addition to the screen capture types, which are the most prom-inent, learning objects come in other forms as well. Tutorials can also be video recordings, slide presentations, animations, or a combination of vari-ous options. Creating a video takes time and preparation. Software consid-erations, creative planning, videotaping or screen captures, and knowledge of editing techniques are required for success. This chapter will provide the information needed to select the best software option and produce a good online tutorial. Creating tutorials can be fun, so embrace the challenge!

Creating Tutorials

The first step to creating tutorials is to establish the overall objective. In-cluded in this early thinking is the affected audience. What exactly is to be conveyed? Who is the audience? Do these concepts fall within the academic environment's educational goals? Lori Mestre, in "Matching Up Learning Styles with Learning Objects: What's Effective?," suggests that consideration should be made for the different types of learning styles of students.[2] She states that tutorials should fulfill "the need to provide a variety of methods that include text, aural, visual, and kinesthetic modalities."[3] Thinking about the target audience and how they might use the tutorials is also a factor. The consistent theme in all tutorial procedure is to plan before jumping into pro-duction. Once determined, these learning objectives and the target audi-ence should be put down in writing. As the tutorial work begins, it is best to design one tutorial for each objective.[4]

Once the objective and audience are determined, choosing the best medium of tutorial creation is the next step. Depending on the outcome de-sired, the overall objective will influence the choice of software or the type of tutorial created. For example, navigating a part of the library website for a database search may be best demonstrated with a screen capture tutorial. However, pitching the value of the library's academic resources may involve a filmed production. If the tutorial needs to be interactive with the student, a corresponding software program should be chosen that allows the students to complete an online quiz or answer a question as they progress through the tutorial. An example of such software would be Camtasia Studio. Will slides, graphs, and other pictures be imported and incorporated into the final production? Will the tutorial need a voice-over? Here too is where thought about ease of use and editing capabilities will influence the medium. These needs influence the choice of medium, which in turn dictates the necessary equipment and software required to create the tutorial.

Securing equipment and software is the third step. Each library will have access to different tools and budget resources. Adapting to these boundaries may require rethinking tutorial methods. Equipment needed may include the appropriate software, microphones, lighting, tripod, and video recorder, all of which have a cost. Many colleges and universities have this equipment, which is made available to librarians and thus would not incur additional spending on the part of the library. While video production software is comprehensive, purchasing of music and a sound effects library may be needed when editing. For filming, some campuses may have a recording studio where audio and video can be produced. Other facilities may create videos in a less formal atmosphere, such as a boardroom or in the library itself. Online software for screen captures and cartoonlike creations are often free. These options require only a computer, microphone plug-in, and Internet access. Other software may provide greater tutorial capabilities but at a cost.

At this point, three steps have been completed—objectives/audience determined, medium selected, and equipment secured. The next step is to actually design the tutorial. Do not start into tutorial creating without a plan! This involves creating the treatment (two-level outlines), storyboard, and scripting. As this process begins, it is good to remember that one- to two-minute tutorials are best.

Both the treatment and storyboard are a rough draft of the online tutorial. It is a plan drawn out of each major segment of the tutorial so that the flow of the recording is laid out. The treatment involves a general overview of the tutorial from beginning to end, and the storyboard breaks down the plan into even smaller scenes.[5] Each part of the storyboard is a scene in the tutorial and may contain descriptive notes of colors, locations, or other details that the drawing may not indicate. Characters, background, objects, and actions should be noted on the sketches. The quality of drawing is not important—use of stick figures and other rough outlines is perfectly fine to indicate the scene. Sometimes simply writing what the scene contains is sufficient.

Storyboard and Script Software

- Atomic Learning's Video StoryBoard Pro
- Storyboard Tools
- Celtx (storyboard and scripting)
- SpringBoard Storyboard Software
- StoryBoard Quick
- Toon Boom Storyboard
- PowerProduction StoryBoard

However, the storyboard should contain enough information that someone reading it can determine what is to be included in each screen shot. Also to be considered are the time spent on each frame, camera angles, lighting needs, sound, and scene transitions. Ideas for infusing graphics and still images should also be noted. Storyboard software is available to assist with this part of the process, if desired.

Either during the storyboard creation or just after it is completed, scripting takes place. Scripting is writing out what is to be said during the tutorial. This part should not be skipped! There are two kinds of scripting—dialogue and shooting.[6] Dialogue script is what will actually be said, and the shooting script describes camera angles, lighting suggestions, and other directions for a video shoot.[7] Whether the tutorial is for a screencast or video with a voice-over, putting down the spoken words in advance is critical. Scripting makes sure the objectives of the tutorial are reached through a clear delivery. Once the dialogue script is in place, it should be reviewed for clarity, flow, and timing. The script should be easily read and practiced by the designated presenter out loud. Often changes to sentence structure and word usage are made when words are spoken rather than simply read. The timing of the script should also take place, and this should match the timing of the storyboard layout. When videotaping, a shooting script considers each individual shot. The use of angles, close-ups, and wide shots should reflect what the viewer would like to see as the dialogue and information unfold.[8] The script and screen shots must match in content and objective. Additionally, the use of secondary scenes may be woven into the video. Ideas for shooting these images should be included in the shooting script. This complementary blending of script and storyboard together will become the final product.

Preproduction steps are important in creating a good tutorial. Determining the objectives and audience ensures that the tutorial will have a focus. Once equipment is secured, creating the storyboard and scripts will take some creative thinking. Several drafts of the tutorial story may be needed. Use library staff to read over the script and offer advice on the storyboard. Remember, this is the foundation the entire tutorial is based upon, so take the time to get it right.

Preproduction Steps

1. Determine objectives and audience
2. Secure equipment
3. Write treatment (outline)
4. Create storyboard
5. Write script

Video Creation

Once the plans, equipment, and script are in place, the video creation begins. A range of options are available from simple screen shot captures to full-blown video filming sets. Which of these the liaison chooses to use depends on the objective, time, and resources available. If the desire is to create a simple tutorial on finding a database on the library website, a screen capture with audio may be best suited. For example, a discussion on the importance of citing copyrighted material may use an animated video option. However, a library tour may involve the use of actual video film production to present a realistic overview. Video production can capture the human element that is missing in the one-way communication of screen capture tutorials.

If the tutorial is simply a screen shot and audio production, screencast software can be utilized. Often these programs can be downloaded for free or at low cost. Typically screen shots and the mouse movements can be captured while narration is delivered with a computer microphone. Depending on the software, editing features such as markups, combined images, transitions, zoom, speed, and resizing are options. The video creator also should check the simplicity of publishing capabilities within the software. Screencast software can be an inexpensive way to create tutorials.

Another inexpensive method of creating a tutorial is through use of an animated video. Once again, no video filming is necessary as the tutorial's objective is carried out through software animation. When opting for animated videos, check the software program for options on theme, background, characters, voices, customization, administrative controls, and music. Typically the script (gestures inserted) is simply typed into the software and when played spoken and acted out by the animated characters. Simple animations of individuals are also an option when liaisons want to animate something they have to say or introduce themselves to the user in a different, fun way. Animated software programs are easy to use and can make an interesting tutorial.

If the tutorial is more complex and involves filming, production includes a video camera, microphones, and lighting. Depending on the equipment available and the storyboard concept, filming a tutorial may involve filming scenes, recording a speaker in existing backgrounds, or recording scenes with music or a voice-over. With some video editing software (such as Adobe Premiere and After Effects), music, transitions, and captions can be added to the production as well. A good example of library videos are those created by Arizona State University (ASU) Libraries and posted to YouTube. View

Screencast Software Options

- Jing
- Snagit
- Screencast-O-Matic
- Screenr
- ScreenToaster
- ALLcapture
- Copernicus
- Snapz Pro X (Mac)
- ShowU (Mac)

Animated Software Options

- Xtranormal
- Voki
- Animoto

ASU's "The Library Minute: My ASU Links" at http://lib.asu.edu/library channel/?cat=87.

Capturing the tutorial video is possible with just one camera and a few good tips. Use of one camera in a straight-on shot is the simplest way to film. However, two or even three cameras can be utilized to film side angles to give a different look to the viewer. Always check exposure, white balance, use a tripod (for stability), and manually focus the video camera for the best shot.[9] (If multiple cameras are in use, the settings of each should be the same.)[10] Regardless of the number, it is advised to keep the camera location the same throughout the shoot.[11] This way the subject and action of the film are in the same location on the film through stops and starts. Some simple filming tips are offered by Todd Stauffer and Nina Parikh, technology and film experts. They suggest the following:

- Have a reason to zoom
- Zoom when the camera is not recording when possible
- Do not talk over a person being interviewed
- Hold the shot a few seconds past the action[12]

In addition to filming the main (or A) roll of film for the tutorial, consider filming secondary (B) shots as well. These secondary shots can be used during an interview sequence to enhance what is being said or to better explain a concept.[13] During the editing process the B-roll can be inserted while the audio track continues to play. For example, if the tutorial is about utilizing study areas in the library, the A-roll could be filming someone talking about study areas and the B-roll could be shots of study rooms, computer labs, or other areas the students use. Use of these creative shots and secondary material during the tutorial should be laid out in the storyboard.

Lighting is the second consideration when filming a tutorial. Lights used for filming should be set up slightly from the side (key light) with a secondary light (fill light) on the other side.[14] A back light from a right or left angle behind the subject can help define the person being filmed and should also be considered.[15] When using lighting, the same light types must be used. All light is rated in degrees Kelvin (color temperatures) and varies depending on type. The use of mixed lighting (such as daylight from a window and lamplight) will not record as well on film and is to be avoided. Available bulb options include incandescent (warmer than daylight), halogen (closer to daylight), fluorescent (daylight colors), hydrargyrum medium-arc iodide (HMI) (sunlight), and light-emitting diodes (LED) (daylight colors).[16] Halogen, fluorescent, and LED bulbs are good options for interview lighting. For convenience, LED lights that are battery operated are now available, eliminating the need for cords. Lighting packages can be purchased (Litepanels, B&M Lighting, BarnDoor Lighting Outfitters, or Lowel-Light Manufacturing) at varying prices. Prices for a light set of three typically begin around $2,000 and include lamps, stands, scrims, barn doors, clamp, cords, and case. This equipment may already be on hand if the college or university has an on-site video lab. A cheaper option is clip-on lights, which may be enough to get started. Depending on the available light, supplemental lighting should match when filming. For example, if good natural light is available, it should be supplemented with a bulb in the spectrum of natural light. If the lighting is in a room that is mixed, block all alternate types of light (such as window light) and use the portable film lights when shooting.

Clear audio is also essential to making a good tutorial video. Use of one or more external microphones, rather than the camera microphone, will produce the best sound results.[17] These microphones can be hand-held, shot-gun (mounted to camera or boom pole), or lavalier (clipped to clothing).[18] The choice of microphone will depend on the camera. A camera for consumer use will have a stereo jack. The professional cameras boast an XRL jack which can handle multiple microphones. Before purchasing a microphone, make sure it matches the camera jack. (Adapters are available if the existing equipment is not compatible.) Eliminate any secondary noises that can be picked up in the sound recording. Finally, wear headphones to listen to the sound coming in and if necessary adjust the audio levels through the camera or a mixing box, if available.[19]

Once the initial track is laid out for the tutorial, editing and evaluation should commence. If the tutorial was filmed, a transfer of the rough footage to editing software takes place. Store the original film in a safe, dry place. Create a rough cut of the scenes that will be used in the final film and save this as well.[20] This is simply an initial cutting out of material from the original footage that will not be used. When editing, be cautious of overusing software transitions for a professional look.[21] Special transitions such as fade or dissolve should indicate a change of location, time, or dramatic motion.[22] During the editing process, a voice-over can be added to the film as well as background music or sound effects. A script for and practice of the voice-over are essential for timing. Sound effects (sonycreativesoftware.com or sound dogs.com) and music (digitaljuice.com or killertracks.com) can be purchased. It is in the editing process that still pictures, graphics, captions, titles, and B-roll film shots will also be inserted. In the editing process, creativity will rule. Allow the audio to continue as scenes change. Use background sounds to enhance the visual work. Finally, close the video with a final scene, montage, narration, or funny closing line and add scrolling credits afterward to complete the tutorial.[23]

Video creation can be as simple as a screen shot with audio or a full-blown video production. Equipment and need will determine exactly which is used. It is at this stage that the script and storyboard are applied to actually making the tutorial. Be prepared for multiple tries (or takes) and the all-important editing stage before the tutorial is finished. Time and patience will deliver an informative video in the end.

Video Creation Checklist

☐ Capturing video
☐ Lighting
☐ Audio/microphones
☐ Software transfer and editing

Software Programs

If the amount of experience or exposure to tutorials is minimal for the library liaison, it can be a good tactic to step back and do exploration about other tutorials and the software available. The liaison may want to access a few library websites and examine their tutorials. It is helpful to note how they were created and what elements of design were the most engaging. Does the tutorial contain a creation method that would suit the project at hand? Hosting options such as library servers, LibGuides, YouTube, and Vimeo should also be considered. Additionally, if technological support is available, it is a good idea for the liaison to contact the information technology (IT) department or instructional technologist. Here there may be help and assistance found for tutorial software. When it comes to the IT department, discussing the project in advance is recommended. The IT staff can offer compatibility suggestions and eventually assist with the installation of new

Low-Cost Tutorial Software Options

- AviScreen
- DemoCreator
- Wink

- iorad
- CamStudio
- ScreenFlow

software. Their help can be invaluable. Often, the IT department has had prior experience with tutorial software and can provide much-needed guidance that can supplement the software company's support staff.

Tutorials were once referred to simply as screencasts. However, software today offers a variety of options from capturing screencasts to complex tutorial productions. (Currently, the two best-known tutorial products are Techsmith's Camtasia and Adobe Captivate, although there are a number of lower-cost options available.) Making things perhaps more complicated in software selection, there are also different formats in which the tutorials can be produced. It can be a very prudent move to download a trial version of the software under consideration before purchasing.

There are a number of considerations when choosing tutorial software. One is how the software allows a tutorial to be created. Some programs record the computer screen and import media files while others require the creation of a video recording.[24] Also, the availability of quiz options should be reviewed. Are a variety of styles available for asking questions of the viewer or are these formats limited? The ability to record mouse actions and keyboard strokes as well as capturing audio simultaneously is yet another consideration. With some software packages, the use of sounds or music is possible. Overall, the objective of the tutorial projects planned for the library should weigh into the final choice of software.

It should be noted that there are a growing number of librarians who are moving away from creating passive tutorials whereby the viewer sits idly by and watches a process, such as accessing a database online. Librarians have also begun to create tutorials that embed hands-on activities so that there will be a greater learning experience when the tutorials are viewed. The insertion of quizzes or questions into the tutorial is one method of increasing interaction. One step beyond that is active tutorial learning provided by simultaneous online tutorial instructions and actively completing steps of a process.

The University of Arizona has developed software specifically for this purpose that contains one box for instructions and questions while an active learning box where the user clicks and moves through activities is open at the same time.[25] This side-by-side instructional software is called Guide on the Side and is now offered as a free download through GitHub. (A direct software link is available at http://code.library.arizona.edu/gots/about and contains a sample tutorial for viewers.)

Using new software typically results in a learning curve for librarians. One of the workarounds that can help with steep learning curves is the feature where software allows the user to begin production using Microsoft PowerPoint. This tactic can be an easy transition for an instruction librarian or library liaison who may already have a repository of presentations that can be quickly converted to tutorials. In its most rudimentary form, a single use can set up a slide show in PowerPoint while the software records the information. That is all that needs to be done, although the addition of an overlaid soundtrack greatly enhances the tutorial.

The price of these most common software products can sometimes be daunting for the average library budget, especially in smaller libraries. As is usual when searching for software, there are lower-priced alternatives and many are open source or free. However, there can be trade-offs relating to the amount of money spent. There are also time limitations, screen size limitations, and embedded advertisements within the free software to consider.

A quick scan through the freely available software that can allow the creation of tutorials shows a wide variety of approaches and file types. There are a number of websites that review the numerous options available Wikipedia (http://en.wikipedia.org/wiki/Comparison_of_screencasting_software) lists over forty versions of screencasting software and sorts them by publisher, latest version, compatible operating systems, licensing, and open source characteristics. There are also some websites that do a good job of giving overviews of some of the more commonly known options available. These sites often list the positive and negative attributes of each software program. For example, MakeUseOf's article "5 Free Screencasting Apps for Creating Video Tutorials" (www.makeuseof.com/tag/5-free-screencasting-apps-for-creating-video-tutorials/) is an excellent resource.[26] A Dream Web Designs blog (http://dreamwebdesigns.com/screencasting-software-comparison-and-features/) offers information on many of the free and retail software programs.[27] Another free option available to the tutorial creator is vendor tutorials and those created by other institutions that may be linked and utilized. Research and study of free and inexpensive programs by the liaison is often necessary to balance tutorial needs with budget restrictions.

A useful, free tutorial resource is the Animated Tutorial Sharing Project (ANTS) (http://ants.wikifoundry.com/). This is a collection of librarian-created content that is openly available for use, reuse, embedding, sharing, or even editing for local needs. Much of their content is available from their YouTube site, known as the Library Information Literacy Online Network or LION TV (www.youtube.com/user/1LIONTV/videos). The purpose of ANTS is to create a place that librarians can come together and share in the development of point-of-need content across institutions. The ANTS website provides information on contributing a tutorial, using existing tutorials, and creating screencasts.[28]

With such a wide range of software programs available, it is important to weigh the content covered, price, quality, and use when making decisions. Library liaisons should take advantage of free trials before making a final decision. Input from fellow librarians and comparative information found on websites will help filter information. Choosing a tutorial software format should be a thoughtful process.

Software Considerations Checklist

- ☐ Recording/creating options
- ☐ Quiz formats
- ☐ Audio options
- ☐ Learning curve
- ☐ Adapting existing tutorials
- ☐ Cost/freeware
- ☐ Trialing software

Additional Considerations

In choosing tutorial software there are some additional considerations. For the disabled students viewing the tutorial, Americans with Disabilities Act (ADA) compliance must be met. Also, software compatibility with platforms and web servers must be reviewed. Finally, the format of file type output options (formats in which the file can be saved) will be affected if the tutorial can not be read by the user's computer or hand-held device. While this chapter will not cover technical services in depth, the library liaison should have an awareness of these various areas that may affect tutorial creation and usage.

ADA compliance in the area of web videos has historically been on a voluntary compliance basis.[29] Because this has been determined to be "insufficient" at the time of this writing, the Department of Justice is considering a rule change to force ADA compliance.[30] Some guidelines are offered by the World Wide Web Consortium (W3C). The W3C emphasizes the use of text equivalents for both audio and visual components because these can be read by the deaf as well as converted into "synthesized speech" for the blind.[31] (Conversely, audio for the text is also of assistance to some users.)[32] Text is easier to read with uppercase and lowercase letters, simple font, and good resolution.[33] When adding the text to the tutorial, it should not cover the visual elements and should match the audio timing.[34] It is also good to keep in mind that some people have color deficiencies. Be sure none of the screencast elements are dependent on color alone.[35] It is easier if software allows ADA-compliant features to be turned on when creating the video, rather than afterward in production. Each software program is different and takes some examination. Perhaps the best course of action is to test tutorials for compliance. This may also be an opportunity to reach out to the academic center's special needs advisor, if available.

When tutorial software is reviewed, compatibility issues must be considered. Is the software available for the computer's platform or operating system? Some software may be available for only a Windows platform and not operable on a Mac platform. Additionally, platforms can become quickly outdated and if the tutorial software works only with a newer version, this should be noted. (Captivate, Camtasia, Jing, and Snagit, for example, are available for use on Windows and Mac OS X systems while Snapz Pro X and QuickTime are created for Mac operating systems.) The version of software also plays a role. For example, Windows 7 operates with Captivate 5.0 or 6.0 but not the 4.0 version. For tutorials being embedded by the liaison librarian into online learning systems, compatibility between the educational and tutorial software must also be checked as well. All software will be hosted by the facility's web server (such as Apache HTTP or Microsoft IIS). This matchup must also be compatible. For example, the 2012 Guide on the Side tutorial software program has been tested on only Apache HTTP servers.[36] As indicated before, checking with technical services before investing time and money into a tutorial program is best.

As mentioned briefly before, tutorial software typically provides a variety of file format options. Depending on how the tutorial will be played by the user, different formats apply. For example, if the tutorial is uploaded to YouTube, MPEG (MPEG-4 with MP3 audio recommended), WebM files, AVI, MOV, MPEGPS, FLV, and WMV are among the accepted formats.[37] Another example is Jing, which offers only an SWF (Shockwave Flash Movie) format in its free version, but for the upgrade to Jing Pro, MP4 video formats are also possible.[38] Once saved in this format, the user would be able to play an SWF tutorial on Adobe Flash Player. An iPad user could play an MPEG-4 video with audio in .m4v, .mp4, or .mov formats as well as JPEG with .avi audio files.[39] (Note that Flash tutorials on mobile devices can be troublesome, so other options should be looked at here.) With each type of software, the file output formats must be reviewed to be sure the format required to be played by the end user is possible.

The end users' ability to utilize the tutorial is what is important. ADA compliance, software and server compatibility, and file formats all play a role in achieving this end. Library liaisons must step into the world of technology in order to achieve success. Formats and programs are constantly changing, so keeping abreast of what is new and developing is essential.

Other Considerations Checklist

☐ ADA compliance (text, audio, descriptions, color)
☐ Platform and server compatibility
☐ File format options

Conclusion

Creating tutorials as a library tool involves preparation through technological research and execution through production steps. Tutorials range from simple to complex and come in screencast, video, and animated forms. Librarians must work through the logistics of software options, ADA compliance, compatibility, and file formats. Additionally, the role of creator takes over through planning, scripting, and filming or capturing ideas. Delivering this wide range of talents is challenging but possible. In the end, assisting the student or faculty member with library information and instruction is the goal. Tutorials are one of the best ways to provide 24/7 service to those who need it!

NOTES

1. Lori Mestre, "Matching Up Learning Styles with Learning Objects: What's Effective?," *Journal of Library Administration* 50, no. 7–8 (2010): 809.

2. Ibid., 808.

3. Ibid.

4. Jonathan Halls, "Creating Videos for Learning," *T+D* (March 2012): 76.

5. Simon Glazebrook, "The Fundamentals of Video Production," *Journal of Visual Communication in Medicine* 33, no. 3 (2010): 118.

6. Ibid.

7. Ibid.

8. Halls, "Creating Videos for Learning," 76.

9. Ibid.

10. Todd Stauffer and Nina Parikh, *Get Creative! The Digital Video Idea Book* (New York: McGraw-Hill, 2003), 76.

11. Ibid., 53.

12. Ibid., 45–48.

13. Ibid., 158.

14. Ibid., 55.

15. Ibid., 102.

16. Videomaker, Inc., "Getting to Know Your On Camera Audio," www.videomaker.com/article/14107/.

17. Halls, "Creating Videos for Learning," 77.

18. Gretchen Siegrest, "Before You Buy a Camcorder Microphone—Buying an External Mic for Your Video Camera," http://desktopvideo.about.com/od/desktopeditinghard ware/bb/externalmic.htm.

19. Videomaker, Inc., "Getting to Know."

20. Glazebrook, "Fundamentals of Video Production," 119.

21. Ibid., 120.

22. Stauffer and Parikh, *Get Creative!*, 220.

23. Ibid., 61.

24. Mestre, "Matching Up Learning Styles," 809.

25. Meredith Farkas, "The Guide on the Side," *American Libraries*, http://americanlibrar iesmagazine.org/columns/practice/guide-side.

26. Travis Quinnelly, "5 Free Screencasting Apps for Creating Video Tutorials," *MakeUseOf*, www.makeuseof.com/tag/5-free-screencasting-apps-for-creating-video -tutorials/.

27. Alan Burchette, "Screencasting Software: Comparison and Features," *Dream Web Designs*, http://dreamwebdesigns.com/screencasting-software-comparison-and -features/.

28. Paul Betty, "Welcome to ANTS," *Library Information Literacy Online Network*, http:// ants.wikifoundry.com/.

29. U.S. Department of Justice, Civil Rights Division, "Nondiscrimination on the Basis of Disability; Accessibility of Web Information and Services of State and Local Government Entities and Public Accommodations" (Washington, DC: Government Printing Office, July 26, 2010) (2010-18334), www.ada.gov/anprm2010/web%20anprm _2010.htm.

30. "Nondiscrimination on the Basis of Disability: Movie Captioning and Video Description," *Regulations.gov*, www.regulations.gov/#!documentDetail;D=DOJ-CRT -2010-0007-0001;oldLink=false.

31. Wendy Chisholm, Gregg Vanderheiden, and Ian Jacobs, eds., "Web Content Accessibility Guidelines 1.0," *World Wide Web Consortium*, www.w3.org/TR/WAI-WEB CONTENT/#Guidelines.

32. Ibid.

33. "Captioning in Camtasia Studio 7," Techsmith Corporation, last updated March 19, 2012, www.svsu.edu/fileadmin/websites/its/itc/Camtasia_Studio/CS_700_Captioning .pdf.

34. Ibid.

35. Chisholm, Vanderheiden, and Jacobs, "Web Content Accessibility Guidelines 1.0."

36. University Libraries, "Guide on the Side," *Arizona Board of Regents for the University of Arizona*, http://code.library.arizona.edu/gots/.

37. YouTube LLC, "Supported YouTube Formats," *YouTube LLC*, http://support.google .com/youtube/bin/answer.py?hl=en&answer=55744.

38. "My Jing Video File Size Is Too Large, How Can I Make It Smaller," *TechSmith Corporation*, http://techsmith.custhelp.com/app/answers/detail/a_id/1122/~/my -jing-video-file-size-is-too-large,-how-can-i-make-it-smaller%3F.

39. "What Is iPad, iPad2 and the New iPad Supported Video & Audio Format?," *Aneesoft Company Ltd.*, www.aneesoft.com/tutorials/ipad-supported-video-format.html#ipad _video_format_supported.

5

Faculty Assistance

The methods of assisting faculty members have changed over time for the library liaison. They have moved from a focus on collection development to more complex tasks. In the Ithaka S+R Report "Faculty Survey 2009: Key Strategic Insights for Libraries, Publishers, and Societies," a good summation of these changes can be used as a starting point for a current approach to working with faculty. The report states the following:

> Faculty used to rely almost exclusively on the library for the scholarly materials they needed for research and teaching, and librarians guided faculty to and otherwise facilitated the discovery of these materials. As scholars have grown better able to reach needed materials directly online, the library has been increasingly disintermediated from research processes. . . . The library must evolve to meet these changing needs. To do so effectively requires awareness of how faculty members evaluate different existing library roles and react to potential changes in library services.[1]

In 2010 Erin Watson added, "As more of our print resources have become available online, fewer faculty are coming to the physical library, which has significantly reduced the amount of face-to-face contact between faculty and librarians."[2] With this knowledge in mind, how does the liaison overcome these hurdles to assist faculty?

In chapter 3, the ability to create relationships with faculty and the importance of these relationships were addressed. In this chapter, the next step in that relationship is reviewing the many ways in which the liaison can assist faculty. Although some of the basics (such as collection development, library policies, services, and available spaces) are outlined elsewhere in this book, as a committed liaison the potential to offer other library assistance to faculty is ever present. This assistance can take many forms, from helping faculty create individual or class web pages to offering research skills for their personal and professional development. Other avenues here include collaboration with faculty in the form of conference presentations, coauthorship, assistance with grant writing, and on-campus or in-service training. In fact, there are no real limitations on how a liaison can contribute to faculty success. In its most ideal form, a mutual relationship with faculty is one in which the liaison librarian assists the faculty member and, through the awareness and promotion of that assistance, gains value within the institution.

Collaboration

All faculty assistance involves collaboration in some form. This varies from a simple give-and-take of information to more complex teamwork. Peggy Pritchard of the University of Guelph Library (Canada) offers three levels of assistance. These are (1) supplementing the curriculum and professor's needs, (2) integrating library skills into individual sessions, and (3) developing and weaving into the curriculum various information literacy skills.[3] Kim Leeder in her blog, *In the Library with a Lead Pipe*, provides another version of collaboration levels. She suggests the simplest level is that of communicating information on student works and needs from library resources.[4] The second level is a cooperative project, such as teaching an IL class, and the third level is through collaborative projects, such as new course creation or grant writing.[5] Looked at from the point of view where collaboration is the ultimate goal, it is easy to see how equality and a shared understanding become a by-product.

It is important to remember that there can be a number of benefits to both parties when collaboration is achieved. For example, in the article "A New Approach to Faculty-Librarian Collaboration: A 'New Professors' Fund' for Collection Development," Tony Horava sets out important attributes of collaboration:

- Mutual goals
- Mutual respect
- Advance planning
- Contributions by both parties[6]

Taking each one of these benefits separately, one can understand how both faculty and librarians can move forward together and maximize their respective skill sets in order to enhance the student's ability to learn and the student experience. Working toward a mutual goal, such as enhancing student research writing with information literacy skills, can bring the liaison and faculty member together as a team. To accomplish this, there must be a degree of mutual respect that adds to the positive relationship and confidence of both parties. The two individuals must plan in advance how they will assist the students. This too will forge the attributes of teamwork and mutual respect. Ultimately, they both contribute to the goal, which brings a sense of accomplishment to both faculty member and library liaison. In this example, the end result would be the improvement of student writing in class research papers. As mentioned in chapter 3, committing to improving communication skills is a great way to foster and nurture relationships. When the librarian does get an opportunity to collaborate with faculty, improve the direct line to students, and influence students' research work, then the result can be classified as a win-win-win.

From a business point of view, faculty could also be considered to be the liaison librarian's clients. With this in mind, a stronger involvement with faculty and direct engagement are imperative. What changes in the faculty and librarian relationship convert a customer or a patron into a client? Peter Hernon, who has championed the need to change the terminology of library patrons to library clients, expresses it this way in an editorial titled "First, Embracing Customer Service and, Second, Moving Beyond It: A Client Relationship."

> Whatever term librarians use to characterize the users of their services merits reconsideration. It should also be appropriate. The term "client," within service content, has some appeal. Can it be applied broadly to the communities using academic libraries? We all know of instances in which the term truly applies. For instance, some programs dealing with information literacy and attracting incoming freshmen classes produce a client relationship. E-reference services may also create a client relationship. If that happens, on-site service should offer a similar relationship.

The question is, "Can the opportunities for a client relationship expand, flourish, and become the norm?"[7]

The realization that there is a need for a different or novel way for the librarian to approach faculty can be liberating, but it can also create its own set of quandaries. Much has been written about faculty and librarian relationships. While some research advises that faculty should be treated as clients, one of the aspects of a client concept is that it implies a hierarchical relationship. The academic institution itself reinforces this concept and often librarians are simply "expert servants."[8] This can be more prominent when the design of the relationship is such that the librarian is classified as staff rather than a full-fledged faculty member. Despite this, the liaison librarian can still view this design positively. One way to subvert, or even embrace, this line of thinking would be to consider Robert K. Greenleaf's concept of servant leadership. Greenleaf posits, "The servant-leader *is* servant first. . . . It begins with the natural feeling that one wants to serve, to serve *first.* Then conscious choice brings one to aspire to lead."[9] Considering that librarians are well accustomed to understanding the importance of service, it is possible for a positive liaison librarian intent on building good faculty relationships to push past any hierarchical barriers.

While there remains resistance in some instances to equality in faculty and liaison collaboration, it has been established that faculty have a positive view of liaisons' efforts to improve communications and awareness of library resources and services. Several studies support this point. Zheng Ye (Lan) Yang writes in her research that "teaching faculty find the library liaison program to be a useful addition to traditional library services."[10] Often positive faculty views are related to the amount of interaction with their library liaison. This has been shown to be the case at both the University of North Carolina–Charlotte's J. Murray Atkins Library and the University of Florida Health Science Center Libraries.[11] In a survey of faculty by Arendt and Lotts, satisfaction with their liaison was indicated by those faculty members who knew the names of their liaison, had been contacted recently by their liaison, and had received services in the past year from their liaison.[12] Collaboration takes active participation by the library liaison to be successful.

One important aspect that is often raised when the subject of assisting faculty is considered is how to manage the time commitment and duties of the librarian. With the duties of the academic liaison expanding, available time is still limited. This dilemma is debated by John Rodwell and Linden Fairbairn of the University of Sydney's Fisher Library who state the following:

> While a dynamic, broader and more intensive role for the Faculty Liaison Librarian is emerging, more thinking is needed about the extent of that role and its sustainability. What, for example, are the priorities for the Faculty Liaison Librarian? What traditional activities can and may have to be abandoned? These considerations are necessary not only to guide the librarians but to help define the attributes and skills required for the position and to determine the institutional support it requires.[13]

Again, different approaches have been used by different campuses to help alleviate this issue. There are some novel or advanced approaches to helping faculty with their research needs. Some libraries create databases or library guides, which are further discussed in chapter 9. These tools are devoted to faculty research and can allow more than one liaison to help as the needs are spread out among many librarians. There are cases where a librarian is designated so that their sole responsibility is to help his or her liaison faculty and others with research needs. In some cases, there can even be a title change or someone besides the liaison librarian does the liaison work. Yet the outcomes are the same when helping faculty with research. These are all ideas to consider when connecting faculty needs to available liaison time.

Many librarians explore the nature of their relationships (or lack thereof) with faculty and approach the situation in different ways. Some can be

Library Intern as Informationist

At Johnson & Wales University–Charlotte, a library intern took on the liaison role of assisting with faculty research. In spring 2011, this intern spent 189 hours compiling 12 research reports on areas of faculty research interests. The reports included pertinent information, sources, citations, and search terms of subject-specific material for faculty members.

SOURCE: Elizabeth A. Thomas, Nora Bird, and Richard J. Moniz, "Informationists in a Small University Library," *Reference & User Services Quarterly* 51, no. 3 (2012): 225.

frustrated while others find that different approaches, such as reinventing the liaison design, can help. Success is found in defining the partnership and collaborative role the liaisons will play. Also, liaisons should have an awareness of the dynamics of the hierarchical academic arena and its impact on the faculty-liaison relationship. Success can be found with active participation and advocating an interactive relationship with faculty while keeping in mind realistic time management goals. Whatever the approach may be to breaking down real or perceived barriers to faculty and librarian collaboration, it is up to the liaison to make a committed and concerted effort to initiate and foster the working relationship in order to provide faculty assistance.

Collaboration Checklist

☐ Work toward mutual goals
☐ Establish a partnership
☐ Consider faculty members as clients
☐ Engage in active participation
☐ Manage demands on time

Types of Assistance

In the effort to collaborate and assist faculty members, liaisons have a variety of methods to utilize. Many of these methods are technology oriented. Librarians are often considered to be at the forefront of emerging technologies. In fact, there are some who have those words in their job titles. Web page creation, database use, and educational software programs are now all included in the realm of the library liaison. Liaisons also can reach out to faculty through research assistance, interlibrary loan services, coauthorship projects, and grant writing. Many liaisons help faculty members make use of institutional repositories as well to highlight and make available their valuable writings and research. These are some of the areas in which liaisons can be of help to the academic professors.

One of the ways librarians can assist faculty is through designing web pages. This can take many forms, from very basic design tips and evaluation all the way up to coding. Web page design has undergone numerous adaptations and transformations since the early days of the Internet. In the past, web page creation was considered an exclusive province for expert programmers.

The domain of difficult-to-learn software programs, such as Microsoft's Front Page, has given way to numerous Web 2.0 tools and sites like Wordpress that make the task simple by comparison. The use of LibGuides (addressed in more detail in chapter 9) is another simple way to assist faculty with information, links, class resources, citation information, copyright help, and technology assistance. The types of web pages created can vary from course to course based on an instructor's needs. Although technology proficiency may not be a requirement of the liaison, acquiring these skills is a plus in assisting faculty in this area.

The liaison has the potential to assist faculty with numerous other technology needs as well. These can include portfolio creation, use of audience response system hardware and software, video creation, and course management software (such as Moodle or Blackboard). For example, at Morehead State University, librarians assisted faculty members with the use of video within their lesson plans.[14] A member of the faculty may need help when creating a personal or class blog or a research portfolio for tenure. As part of library instruction classes, the library liaison can assist faculty with the use of audience response systems for student feedback. Many liaisons will gain experience in the use of class management software that allows the instructor to control the students' computers in a lab. This experience can also be used to help faculty use these types of systems and incorporate this learning tool into their presentations.

Library liaisons can also assist faculty with their understanding of new hardware, such as e-readers and tablets. They can suggest new software functions that could enhance teaching presentations. Examples include Pinterest (online pinboard), Prezi (presentation software), Edublogs (online blogs), Wikispaces (online wiki), and Testcraft (test creator). The possibilities for technology help requests are actually somewhat limitless and can change rather quickly. This is why it is a good idea for librarians to have a basic awareness of any new technology and pedagogies so that they may be at the forefront of the faculty's minds when help is needed.

Although there is overlap with reference and instruction responsibilities, the liaison should have a good grasp of the fundamental design and functions of the library databases should questions arise. It is an academic library ritual to reassess library databases during the summer and proceed to make changes in the form of additions and subtractions. This impels the librarian to be aware of new offerings as the new school year begins and can make a large

impact on librarian perception when a flashy or much-needed function of a
new relevant resource is pointed out to faculty and students. Faculty can use
their knowledge of newly purchased databases and their functions to direct
students to them and use them themselves when doing research.

Interlibrary loan (ILL) is a time-honored service of the academic library.
Put simply, it is a service wherein librarians offer access to many more resources than those available at the local institution. These are often thought
to be books, yet document retrieval is a very large part of ILL. Through library
agreements, one can borrow from many other institutions through previously
defined agreements. The use of ILL has been steadily on the increase—up 54
percent from 1998 to 2008—making it a critical component for resource assistance.[15] Many libraries have staff members who have either primary or sole
responsibility to take care of ILL requests. These services can assist faculty
with research documents for personal study as well as their students seeking
information for classes. Depending on the policies and procedures implemented on your campus, there can be different ways that ILL is presented to
faculty and carried out. Some institutions use their own request forms and
paper forms for tracking. Others use more automated systems, such as OCLC's
ILLiad. Whatever the method used, securing off-site documents has become
an important feature in assisting faculty.

It can be difficult to promote how extensive ILL resource availability is to
a faculty member, but once the message has been received, there are often
innumerable requests. An example of this at McGrath Library at Hilbert
College is detailed here:

> During the past few years, McGrath Library implemented a liaison pro-
> gram to improve its relationship with faculty. Through this program,
> librarians communicate more frequently with faculty in their specific
> subject areas. The use of ILL by faculty has increased since this program
> was put in place. Awareness has led more faculty to think of ILL as an
> option to them, and they are more likely to take advantage of the service.[16]

Margaret H. Bean and Miriam Rigby document how the University of Oregon
focused on their ILL marketing and procedural problems by creating what
they described as "a successful in-house outsourcing program between
University of Oregon Library departments."[17] They fostered collaboration
between interlibrary loan staff and subject specialists (or liaisons) to expe-
dite faculty ILL requests and, additionally, used this partnership to help with

requests in which the materials were difficult to find. ILL is an important method of assistance that liaisons give to faculty members.

Faculty assistance can also take place in a number of other ways. Co-authorship with a faculty member on a research paper is one of these. Assistance with background research for a grant application can be of great help to a faculty member as well. In-service training sessions and conference proceedings offer innumerable opportunities for faculty and librarians to work together through joint presentations. Because faculty members are often working on personal degrees and research projects, the librarian is often considered a valuable research resource. Faculty members may call upon the liaison they have connected with for research help on occasion. Some libraries specifically designate a staff member or several to help all faculty members with research. Liaisons should actively seek out these many opportunities to assist faculty and become involved when possible.

One other specific area in which librarians can help with faculty research needs is providing overviews and help with citation management software or tools and reference management software. Citation management software such as Zotero, RefWorks, EasyBib, and EndNote can provide efficient methods for collecting sources used when compiling research and also help with citation construction and proper use. Some of the reference management software overlaps with citation help, but it can also be a great benefit for researchers when collecting information. Products such as Zotero and Mendeley make finding and collecting research resources easier than do more rudimentary methods, such as a spreadsheet or a document, and even offer the ability to collaborate and find the most cited or popular information.

Last, institutional repositories are relatively new in their popularity and offer yet another way for the librarian to reach out to and assist faculty. Often these are local online digital collections and archives of documents such as dissertations, conference papers, research papers, and other pertinent academic information related to an institution. These give colleges and universities the opportunity to collect and share research and other information with whoever is deemed to be given access. The faculty may not be aware of this resource as a way to archive, collect, and publicize their research work. Tied into archiving research is showcasing this work. One way librarians can accomplish this is by offering a lecture series. Justine Cotton and Heather Pfaff of Brock University Library (Ontario, Canada) planned and hosted a lecture series featuring faculty talking about their current research because "the library has an important role to play not only in providing researchers with information, but also in celebrating the research achievements on campus."[18] Often these are open access and open source document databases. It can fall on the academic librarians to be collectors, catalogers, and trainers of these repositories.

There are a variety of ways to assist faculty as an academic liaison. Technological assistance through web pages, databases, and software programs plays an increasing role in both creating information resources as well as assisting with educational aids. Copyright and citation assistance is often needed by faculty members. Additionally, liaisons utilize interlibrary loan to help faculty with both personal and class-related research needs. Sometimes research assistance ties into coauthorship opportunities. Finally, archiving faculty writings and research projects through an institutional repository is of great help. These activities give the liaison a long list of ways to connect and assist the academic professionals.

Assistance Checklist

- ☐ Web page creation
- ☐ Database and software resources
- ☐ Interlibrary loan
- ☐ Research, authorship, grant assistance
- ☐ Citation management
- ☐ Institutional repositories

Classroom Teaching Assistance

The library liaison has a unique opportunity to work in tandem with faculty when creating assignments for the classroom. Opportunities here are often available through assessing the research aspects of assignments and assisting in the online learning forum. In some instances, liaison librarians become coteachers of the class. Typically, faculty may agree to let the librarian help with certain aspects of a course or class. However, it can be the preconceived notions of a faculty member that define the librarian's role, which in turn dictates the librarian's initial duties and responsibilities as a collaborative teacher. There have been observations that show that even the basic conceptualization of librarians as teaching partners is one-sided, librarian-driven, and rarely enters into the minds of faculty.[19] Despite this, there have been and continue to be many instances where librarians and teaching faculty come together to teach.

As mentioned previously, hierarchical relationships between faculty members and librarians have existed in the academic world. Faculty members regard themselves as higher status because of their education and tenure status. In some instances, tenure is extended to librarians. The Association of College and Research Libraries recommends that tenured librarians be equal to faculty in areas of rank, compensation, sabbaticals, research funds, and other applicable policies.[20] There can be such categories as librarians with faculty status and tenure, with faculty status but no tenure, without faculty status but with status similar to tenure, and without faculty status at all. There are also other positions that more closely align with the designation of "staff." Because of these distinctions, faculty often have preconceptions and ideas about librarians. Their interest in becoming teaching partners is often influenced by faculty status views. In a blog post titled "Comrades-in-Arms: The Professor and the Librarian," Rochelle Mazur sums up these feelings succinctly:

> We want the teaching faculty (and by this I mean anyone from the rank of associate professor on up) to see us as their equals, as comrades-in-arms in the daily battle to produce good scholarship, excellent graduates, and better the general welfare of our shared institution and Knowledge in general. We want a standing invitation to the faculty club. We don't want to be seen as *the help*.[21]

Although it can be argued that viewing and treating someone as an equal should not be completely dependent upon anything more than shared goals, as Mazur states, often reality is just that—the librarians are simply "the help." Irene Doskatsch, senior information librarian at the University of South Australia, Adelaide, suggests librarians "shed their preconceptions about how academics and librarians should collaborate and accept shared responsibility for student learning."[22] Whatever the librarian's position may be in relation to rank and title, there are cases where coteaching does take place.

One of the forms of coteaching exists in the online classroom. More so than in any other role, the library liaison can assist students in an online environment when helping faculty with classes. Although this subject is discussed in chapter 8, "Embedded Librarianship," it can also be mentioned and introduced here. There are numerous ways to help an instructor with online learning. These range from providing some technical help, to offering

assignment support, and even the opportunity to participate in a coteaching role within the class. A novel approach is the one used at University of
Maryland University College where librarians designed online training workshops for faculty especially focused on incorporating information literacy
into classroom assignments.[23] Once trained, faculty can then team up with
liaisons to ensure students are learning critical information literacy tools.

As a touchstone for liaisons to present their value to faculty in the process of research assignment design, one need look no further than the results
found in the July 2010 Project Information Literacy Progress Report titled
"Assigning Inquiry: How Handouts for Research Assignments Guide Today's
College Students." This report studied 191 course-related research assignments on 28 United States campuses and determined that handouts for these
assignments were more about how to prepare the assignment than recommending research guidance and information resources.[24] Because it is the
librarian's forte, the liaison can offer advice on how to craft an assignment
that will return better-researched projects. In fact, faculty-librarian collaboration with these skills can ease students' anxiety when it comes to research
projects.[25] Two of the tactics used can be (1) taking into consideration that
the students have minimal library knowledge and skills and (2) including
research steps within the assignment. Additionally, library liaisons can help
in the classroom by suggesting ideas for clearly defined assignments and
strategies for narrowing topics. For example, a student might begin a search
using a term such as "prison reform" and be inundated with numerous search
results. The librarian can suggest trying similar keywords such as "criminal
justice," "incarceration," and "detention" to help with too few or too general

Assignment Composition Tips

- Include resource quality as part of the grade
- Provide quantity and quality of resources expected
- Provide a preliminary resource list
- Review cited, quoted, and paraphrased material
- Provide sample topics

SOURCE: University of California Berkeley Library, "Effective Research Assignments,"
Regents of the University of California, www.lib.berkeley.edu/instruct/assignments.html.

results or adding additional narrowing terms such as "prison reform" and "North Carolina" or "prison reform" and "effect on children." These suggestions can alleviate the frustration of too many results during the search process. The University of Texas Libraries website helps faculty when creating effective research assignments by suggesting that the assignment should define the terms used. For example, terms such as "peer-reviewed articles" or "primary resources" need to be defined within the assignment.[26]

Given the opening to help with assignment creation for a class, the librarian can be an added value because he or she can tailor the research requirements so that students can meet with the greatest chance of success. Having an advantage due to a wide understanding of resources available, the librarian gives the students a "leg up" when it comes to making sure that the library has relevant resources and diminishes the possibility of frustration. Additionally, the librarian can also map out specific resources or possibly instruct students in ways to meet with the greatest success when looking for assignment information. And last, when the librarian uses a welcoming manner, the students will see the librarian as approachable, which can also help them receive good grades on their research work. With these tactics, the liaison can work in many different ways to offer assistance with assignments, which can be associated with instruction whether formal class instruction (lecture) is done by the librarian or not.

Assignment Alternatives

- Compare and contrast a peer-reviewed article, website, and popular magazine
- Create an annotated bibliography on a topic
- Compile a list of search terms (use library reference desk as needed)
- Present and give examples of the numerous types of resources available
- Create a list of hot topics in the field
- Analyze websites versus peer-reviewed sources for bias

SOURCE: Folke Bernadotte Memorial Library, "Suggestions for Assignments," *Gustavus Adolphus College*, https://gustavus.edu/library/IMLS/assignmentsuggestions.html.

Whether in an online learning environment or in the classroom, once given the green light to help with pointing the students to library and other information sources, the library liaison can often take on the role of coteacher. If the librarian is involved in assignment creation, it is important to think "outside the library" and take the opportunity to make students aware of all of the resources available to them, not just sanctioned library resources. Assisting faculty in the areas of technology as well as assignment creation enhances information literacy learning opportunities for the student. Liaisons can be more than just assistants to faculty; they can become educators!

Classroom Teaching Assistance Checklist

☐ Technical assistance
☐ Assignment support
☐ Research project design
☐ Information literacy integration

Conclusion

With online resources so prevalent, faculty visits to the library are often limited. Library liaisons must take an active role in reaching out to these educators in order to assist with classroom learning. While barriers still exist in the areas of status, liaison librarians are taking on ever-increasing roles in coteaching. Assistance with technology, educational software, database usage, research materials, and grant writing is an important role of the liaison. Additionally, integrating information literacy skills in the classroom, both in person and online, plays a critical role in student learning. This help with assignment and course delivery has steered the liaison into the realm of educator and coteacher. This is the path that lies ahead for many library liaisons. It is time to assist!

NOTES

1. Roger C. Schonfeld and Ross Housewright, "Faculty Survey 2009: Key Strategic Insights for Libraries, Publishers, and Societies," *Ithaka S+R*, www.sr.ithaka.org/research-publications/faculty-survey-2009: 8.

2. Erin M. Watson, "Taking the Mountain to Mohammed: The Effect of Librarian Visits to Faculty Members on Their Use of the Library," http://ecommons.usask.ca/

bitstream/handle/10388/377/New%20review%20of%20academic%20librarianship%20--%20post-print.pdf?sequence=3.

3. Peggy Pritchard, "Reinventing Science Librarianship Posters on Display," www.docstoc.com/docs/26542136/Reinventing-Science-Librarianship-Posters-on-Display.

4. Kim Leeder, "Collaborating with Faculty Part 2: What Our Partnerships Look Like," *In the Library with the Leadpipe* (blog), www.inthelibrarywiththeleadpipe.org/2011/collaborating-with-faculty-part-2-what-our-partnerships-look-like/.

5. Ibid.

6. Tony Horava, "A New Approach to Faculty-Librarian Collaboration: A 'New Professors' Fund' for Collection Development," *Journal for Academic Librarianship* 31, no. 5 (2005): 482.

7. Peter Hernon, "Editorial: First, Embracing Customer Service and, Second, Moving Beyond It: A Client Relationship," *Journal of Academic Librarianship* 28, no. 4 (2002): 189.

8. Kristin Anthony, "Reconnecting the Disconnects: Library Outreach to Faculty as Addressed in the Literature," *College & Undergraduate Libraries* 17, no. 1 (2010): 81–82.

9. Robert K. Greenleaf, *The Power of Servant Leadership* (San Francisco, CA: Berrett-Koehler, 1998), 1.

10. Zheng Ye (Lan) Yang, "University Faculty's Perception of a Library Liaison Program: A Case Study," *Journal of Academic Librarianship* 26, no. 2 (2000): 128.

11. Michele R. Tennant and Tara Tobin Cataldo, "Development and Assessment of Specialized Liaison Library Services," *Medical Reference Services Quarterly* 21, no. 2 (2002): 34; Julie Arendt and Megan Lotts, "What Liaisons Say about Themselves, and What Faculty Say about Their Liaisons, a U.S. Survey," *Libraries and the Academy* 12, no. 2 (2012), www.press.jhu.edu/journals/portal_libraries_and_the_academy/portal_pre_print/current/articles/12.2lotts.pdf: 158.

12. Arendt and Lotts, "What Liaisons Say about Themselves."

13. John Rodwell and Linden Fairbairn, "Dangerous Liaisons? Defining the Faculty Liaison Librarian Service Model, Its Effectiveness and Sustainability," *Library Management* 29, no. 1–2 (2008): 116.

14. Ray Bailey, Gina Blunt, and Monica Magner, "Librarian and Faculty Collaboration on Video Projects," *Kentucky Libraries* 75, no. 1 (2011): 16–18.

15. Denise M. Davis, "Trends in Academic Libraries, 1998–2008," *American Library Association*, www.ala.org/research/sites/ala.org.research/files/content/librarystats/academic/ALS%209808%20comparison.pdf: 12.

16. Elizabeth Curry, "Little Changes to Interlibrary Loan Services Make a Big Difference at a Small Academic Library," *Journal of Interlibrary Loan, Document Delivery & Electronic Reserve* 19.4 (2009): 287–90.

17. Margaret H. Bean and Miriam Rigby, "Interlibrary Loan Reference Collaboration: Filling Hard-to-Find Faculty Requests," *Journal of Interlibrary Loan, Document Delivery and Electronic Reserve* 21, no. 1 (2011): 1.

18. Justine Cotton and Heather Pfaff, "The Secret Lives of Professors: Connecting Students with Faculty Research through a Faculty Lecture Series," *Feliciter* 55, no. 6 (2009): 254.

19. Lars Christiansen, Mindy Stombler, and Lyn Thaxton, "A Report on Librarian-Faculty Relations from a Sociological Perspective," *Journal of Academic Librarianship* 30, no. 2 (2004): 117.

20. Committee on the Status of Academic Librarians, "A Guideline for the Appointment, Promotion and Tenure of Academic Librarians," *Association of College & Research Libraries*, www.ala.org/acrl/standards/promotiontenure.

21. Rochelle Mazur, "Comrades-in-Arms: The Professor and the Librarian," *Random Access Mazar: From the Trenches of Librarianship* (blog), http://randomaccessmazar .wordpress.com/2005/09/18/comrades-in-arms-the-professor-and-the-librarian/.

22. Irene Doskatsch, "Perceptions and Perplexities of the Faculty-Librarian Partnership: An Australian Perspective," *Reference Services Review* 31, no. 2 (2003): 119.

23. Robert Miller et al., "Library-Led Faculty Workshops: Helping Distance Educators Meet Information Literacy Goals in the Online Classroom," *Journal of Library Administration* 50, no. 7–8 (2010): 830.

24. Alison J. Head and Michael B. Eisenberg, Project Information Literacy Progress Report, "Assigning Inquiry: How Handouts for Research Assignments Guide Today's College Students," *The Information School, University of Washington*, http://projectinfolit .org/pdfs/PIL_Handout_Study_finalvJuly_2010.pdf: 1.

25. Mara L. Houdyshell, "Navigating the Library: What Students (and Faculty) Need to Know," *College Teaching* 51, no. 2 (2003): 76.

26. "Creating Effective Research Assignments," *University of Texas Libraries*, www.lib .utexas.edu/services/instruction/faculty/creatassignment.html.

Collection Development

Many different job titles are associated with collection development, but per-haps none more so than that of the library liaison. One of the historical foun-dations of library liaison work is rooted in the area of collection development and supporting the various subjects taught by the academic institution. As early as 1949, Herman Fussler, director of the University of Chicago Library, described the need for subject bibliographers (the modern library liaison) as follows:

> He must know books, book values, dealers, and dealers' specialties . . . he
> must enjoy reading dealers' catalogs and examining secondhand books;
> he must know the faculty of his area and what they are working upon; he
> must know where their judgment of books can supplement his and where
> it is apt to be deficient.[1]

As it was in the late 1940s, a liaison of today still serves a pivotal role in connecting faculty as well as students to the library's collections. These librarians are involved in administering collection development through set policies. Additionally, library liaisons handle both suggestions and requests for the collection development as well as subject-related acquisitions. To accomplish this, familiarity with the budgetary process, accountability, and budget formulas is also important. While the methods and materials of a library liaison have changed greatly, collection development remains a core task of these specialists.

Collection Development Policies

It is especially important for library liaisons to be familiar with the library's collection development policies and purchasing procedures. Collection development principles also often require ongoing debate among the liaisons and other relevant library staff. They typically address the relative place for requests in terms of collection development and place emphasis on what kinds of requests might be favored over others. Whether or not the library will collect foreign language materials or do any retrospective purchasing may also be a part of this discussion. Other issues might include whether or not duplication should be sought in certain areas or whether or not the library will provide students access to textbooks and, if so, under what circumstances. These policies and procedures can vary considerably from one institution to the next. However, the most common policies contain some form of each of the following elements: the library's overall mission, objectives for developing the collections, assignment of responsibility, criteria for selection, principles for collecting resources, specific descriptions of what collections consist of, a gift policy, fund allocation specifics, and quite often a policy for weeding materials from the collection. Once determined, it is important for the liaison to be familiar with this document and, when possible, actively assist in crafting or adapting it as appropriate and necessary.

If the library's mission has been crafted well, it will tie directly into that of the parent college or university. This has both direct and indirect implications for collection development. For example, if an institution states that it will be a premier educator in electrical engineering, it is obvious that those collections or access to resources relevant to this area will be important. In a more indirect way, a role that indicates "support for research" or a similar inclination suggests much more comprehensive collections and access to resources than a program that may support only "hands-on learning." Collection objectives often flow logically from the library mission statement in making these commitments more concrete. A mission statement might indicate the need to maintain a certain high level of collections in a specific area or to support specific programs or classes. For example, the Harvard Law School Library mission statement states, "The Library acquires, catalogs, preserves and makes available a world-class collection of both contemporary and historical legal materials."[2] The objectives may then specify further what this means in terms of total volumes held or ability to conduct in-depth research. At Harvard, programs and curriculum mandate collecting and preserving legal documents from Afghanistan, collecting but not preserving documents from Belize, and relying on only digital access for those from France.[3] This is an example of collection development objectives broken down into very specific components.

Assignment of subject responsibility for collection development can vary considerably from one institution to the next as well. That said, it is fairly common for a college or university to assign a librarian to a specific program area or set of areas. This is in fact a central role for anyone serving as a liaison. While communicating with faculty regarding teaching courses is critical (as has been stated many times over in this book), many faculty will view the liaison primarily from the perspective that these librarians are the ones who can get them the information sources needed for both their own research and that of their students. Collection development documents often specify these arrangements in conjunction with other collection development components, discussed below.

Determining the criteria for selecting materials often involves discussion among library staff, sometimes in consultation with relevant faculty. Criteria for selection may include the following:

- Relevance of subject matter to the curriculum and to the university's or college's mission
- Currency of material
- Authoritativeness of material as reflected in reviews or as reflected in other sources deemed reliable by subject area selectors
- Author's or editor's scholarly or professional reputation
- Permanency of material
- Contribution to the balance of collections
- Reputation of the publisher
- Price

While these criteria are fairly straightforward, they do involve some qualitative judgments and questions to be considered. What is relevant to the mission? What is current in one field, and does a particular date or currency differ for another? (For example, a business major might need the most current economic data whereas a history major might want an authoritative text dating back many years.) Which reviews are most reliable? How does one determine the author's or the publisher's reputation? How expensive is the resource? Is the item or resource low cost with potentially little use or high cost but potentially a critical need? The liaison should apply the best criteria to improve the collection for their respective subject areas.

Specific descriptions of the collections will build on principles and other criteria as established to inform the liaison as to specific rules and guidelines when engaging in collection development. For example, a library liaison of an institution offering a culinary degree would specialize in collecting cookbooks, periodicals, and culinary database resources. The collection development policy would guide this liaison on how to make these choices. A history liaison may collect historical videos and the policies specify the kinds of circumstances under which a DVD might be purchased to fill a classroom need. This area of the collection development policy might also specify that a particular type of resource is not collected. An example of this might be VHS tapes (as they have become obsolete) or print indexes that lack any full text. Again, the specifics of the collection principles depend on the nature of the institution.

Libraries almost always have an established gift policy associated with broader collection development policies. Liaisons need to know what the gift policy is and be able to share it with others outside the library. A typical policy will give wide latitude to the library staff to determine what types of donations may or may not be included in the collection. This is important because as the liaison interacts with faculty, they may be offered books or other materials. A mistake would be to take the material, not be able to include it in the collection, and then at a later date have a faculty member upset that it has not been included and perhaps even discarded or sold in a book sale. Informing the faculty member up front of a gift policy that indicates not all materials will be included in the collection can prevent any misunderstandings in this regard.

Funding for collections not only involves discussion; it can also involve heated debate. Since the library has only so much money in a materials line item or items adding to one area, this almost always means sacrifices somewhere else. Liaisons can be in a difficult spot as they may need to advocate for specific program areas but also recognize the need for compromise with liaisons covering other areas as well. Often the principles of collection development that have been established as a guide for this discussion can be useful. However, it should be stated that this too is an area worth building a bridge with faculty. A library committee with faculty representation, for example, could determine how resources are to be allocated. While still based on recommendations put forth by the librarians, this gives the faculty an opportunity to share concerns, allows them to buy into collection-related decisions, and often turns them into advocates for adequate library resource funding. The liaison's role is to advocate for his or her subject areas while understanding the need to balance available funds across all academic subjects.

Weeding a collection can also be more challenging than it might first appear. Liaisons need to be familiar with what faculty and students actually use. When library shelf space is not as big of a concern, one might lean toward being more conservative in the weeding process. When space is an issue one might lean toward being more aggressive in removing items that are out of date or no longer relevant. The library's integrated library system (ILS) can be helpful in creating lists of which items have been checked out and which have not. Vendors also regularly provide usage data as well. Library liaisons are expected to analyze this information and make qualitative judgments about what should be kept in the collection and what is removed.

In the end, the overall assessment of the collections will allow for the collection development policy to be updated and specific collection targets to be met. Keep in mind that as institutions change, so must this document. As mentioned elsewhere in this book, the addition of new program areas can be an especially significant concern. For example, academic centers focused on fostering research may utilize the statistics published by the Association of Research Libraries. These statistics include "collections, expenditures, service activities, staffing, and salaries" and can be matched against one's own institution.[4] This could be especially helpful in both determining the current adequacy of the collection and assessing the future direction of development.[5] Vendors such as Baker and Taylor can assist as well. For example, their core titles lists available online provide library liaisons with a ready list of general titles as well as those for specific areas of study. According to the Yankee Book Peddlers (YBPs) website, "The titles selected are carefully screened to identify major titles that will stand the test of time, which would be considered standard (core) works in any good undergraduate collection."[6] Another example would be the WorldCat Collection Analysis tool. According to WorldCat,

> To make the most of your acquisitions budget, you need precise data
> that reveals your library's subject-matter strengths, gaps, and overlaps.
> WorldCat Collection Analysis lets you analyze your collection and com-
> pare it to other collections without requiring you to expend extensive
> staff, time, or financial resources.[7]

Usage patterns from a library's own ILS and annual survey instruments can also be helpful in this regard.

The library liaison's involvement in collection development requires applying the collection policies and criteria to their specific subject areas. In growing the collection, the selection criteria must tie in to the library's mission, which ultimately supports the academic center's mission as well. Collection descriptions can assist library liaisons, especially those new to collection development, with how to develop their specific areas. Often included in the collection cycle of purchase, use, and weeding is the negotiating for budgetary dollars. The library liaison must also have an idea of what is useful in the collection through both statistics and qualitative judgments so updates to the collection policy base can be made as the library moves forward.

Collection Development Checklist

☐ Collecting in step with the library mission
☐ Criteria for selection and handling gifts
☐ Specific collection descriptions
☐ Advocating for funding
☐ Determining how the collection moves forward

Suggestions/Requests

The library liaison must determine a way to handle suggestions and requests. While there may be a system in place, liaisons are usually given some flexibility in this regard. Suggestions and requests, while similar, are handed differently. Suggestions are possible additions to the collections while requests are classified as necessary materials. Suggestions and requests could come from any number of areas and be given weight accordingly. For example, in the area of accreditation, acting upon recommendations for additions to the collection by accrediting teams might be given a very high priority. Likewise, suggestions by faculty members who need materials for a class might also be very important to follow up on. Such opportunities for suggestions can be almost never-ending. While challenging, these suggestions do direct library liaisons toward items of interest.

Although they can obviously overlap, a suggestion is differentiated from a request just as a want from a need. A request would be more reflective of a *specific need*. Suggestions are not. It is important to consider the distinction. Sometimes faculty, administrators, or accrediting teams will offer possibilities or ideas for adding to the collection that do not address a need as such. Suggestions may include a faculty member's interest in a new art book that was mentioned in a recent book review. This is more of a suggestion, and the library liaison would explore or further evaluate the actual value of this addition. Requests usually imply that a faculty member intends to use specific materials or resources. For example, the liaison might get a request for a book, database, or other resource that will be used for a specific assignment in a specific class or classes from a faculty member, student, or academic department chair. The liaison must determine how to classify the suggested material before proceeding with a possible purchase.

The system for handling these suggestions and requests can vary considerably. One might move suggestions for less expensive items directly over to purchasing and direct more expensive items for discussion with the chair of a given department or even a library committee as a whole. Sometimes asking faculty members to affix a priority number (such as 1 for extreme need, 2 for supplemental material, or 3 for a nice-to-have addition) can help a liaison sort through the suggestions. One might also consider historically which purchases have been made for a given faculty member or area. While these methods of handling relate to one-time purchases, fixed or ongoing expenses such as periodical subscriptions and database subscriptions might vary. Since they are billed to the library each year, they cut into future discretionary spending.

It is the job of the library liaison to get suggestions for holdings. Some faculty will be regulars in placing requests. However, it is often important to get creative in order to get requests from a wider range of people. For example, one idea would be to drop a postcard into each faculty member's mailbox asking them to send it back with a request for five specific items. Each participant could then be placed in a raffle for a gift card. As stated many times earlier, building relationships with faculty is critical. These relationships

should pay dividends in the area of specific requests as well. Beyond referrals from faculty or accreditation teams, liaisons can also tap into ALA and
vendor resources. If one attends an ALA Annual Conference or an ACRL
Biannual Conference, the opportunity exists for suggestions for the addition of numerous resources. The ALA and ACRL websites are great places to
visit for more information as well in this regard. Vendors such as Ebrary and
YBP (just to name a couple of common companies that libraries frequently
work with) also have systems for sharing suggested new publications with
regular customers based on preestablished profiles. These can be very useful
for a liaison and associated faculty, allowing them to see items right when
they become available. In fact, some libraries have made this type of system
the central component of their requesting procedures. At Dalton State College
they utilize Midwest Library Service's New Book Selection Service to send
out information about new materials being published to the faculty by e-mail.
They have found this system to be highly successful in involving more faculty
members in the process of collection development.[8] Utilization of vendors is
an excellent source for suggested subject specialty additions to the collection.

As stated earlier in this book, the collection will not develop appropriately
if the liaison simply sits back and waits for suggestions or requests. In fact,
that would be one way to imbalance the collection as certain information
sources and areas may produce more suggestions and requests than others.
Liaisons must be involved in active solicitation of these collection ideas. As
stated, it is important to know the needs of the students and faculty and the
resources that are available. Staying on top of trends, though, goes beyond
just the here and now. It is important to forecast what will occur in the future.
One might attend programs such as the one conducted at the ALA's 2012
Annual Conference, sponsored by the Library Leadership and Management
Association (LLAMA), titled "Future Quest: Creating a Vision for Academic
Libraries." Here, data and discussion are highlighted, among other relevant
points. Currently, there is a greater desire by users for access to e-books and
a greater emphasis on the need for librarians and library administrators to
better utilize online social networks to connect with important constituencies. LLAMA will undoubtedly be at the forefront of sharing similar data in
the future. In addition to conferences, workshops, and webinars, a number
of periodicals seek to address trends and specific resources. *Library Journal*
and *Choice: Current Reviews for Academic Libraries* are a couple of different examples. Other more scholarly journals, such as *College & Research*

Libraries or *College & Undergraduate Libraries* or *The Acquisitions Librarian* might also contain relevant implications for collection development based on studies of user needs and other elements. Networking with liaisons at other institutions is yet another way one could stay ahead of the curve. Library liaisons must be constantly searching new publications for relevant topics to enhance the collection.

Part of the liaison job is to sort through specific requests and suggestions for materials. They must determine which are of most importance to supporting academic needs. This area of collection suggestions and requests includes those recommended by faculty, administration, and accrediting bodies but also goes beyond the boundaries of the academic institution. Liaisons must actively seek out new materials through attendance at library conferences and their associated webinars as well as through vendors. Library liaisons must have their pulse on all of these various sources for collection ideas in order to select and provide the best resources possible.

Suggestions and Requests Checklist

- ☐ Determining suggestions versus requests
- ☐ Utilizing referrals, ALA conferences, vendors
- ☐ Active collecting

Acquisitions

The acquisition of new materials and resources has obvious ties to the aforementioned policies and ideas related to collection development. While the collection development policy lays out what and why for collection development, acquisitions deals more with the how. Acquisitions include the ordering process (both one-time and periodical purchases), database selection, and print versus electronic analysis.

Ordering processes can differ considerably from one institution to the next. That said, it makes sense to streamline this process as much as possible for a number of reasons. A streamlined process requires less processing work by library staff (thus allowing more time to be dedicated to other liaison activities) and also allows a better response time. This can be achieved largely by working with specific vendors. For example, a library might have an account with YBP, Ingram, or other such entity whereby it may acquire print materials through a central database and ordering system. These vendors often offer substantial discounts and other services as well. If ordering directly, the liaison may need to acquire a user name and password and become familiar with the vendor's database and ordering system. The liaison might also need to separately track spending using the ILS or an Excel spreadsheet. It is worth noting that not all materials can be purchased this way. While most items may be available through a licensed vendor or vendors and other common items handled through sites such as Amazon.com, faculty will frequently seek special materials that may be made available only from a specific company or source. In such cases, the library liaison must be familiar with the purchasing process at his or her institution. At larger colleges or universities, the library may have its own acquisitions department. In other circumstances, the library may require assistance from a separate purchasing department that handles purchase orders and accounts payable. In this latter case, it may be necessary to familiarize oneself with the paperwork or process followed for buying items from atypical vendors. These methods typically reflect a one-time purchase.

For print periodicals, the acquisitions process usually differs. A consideration needs to be made when subscribing to periodicals that this may be a long-term commitment. Thus, funds will need to be allocated not just in the current fiscal year but in future years as well. This has obvious implications for library budgeting. Even a small library will typically utilize a vendor to assist it in handling print periodicals. For example, EBSCO's EBSCONET and subscription management service can help manage payment of fees to all periodicals subscribed to for an additional service fee.[9] This service can be well worth the cost when one considers the potential need for hundreds of separate checks to be written to each publisher at different times throughout the year. Once selected, periodical purchases will typically be an ongoing budget item for the library.

Databases are yet another area for consideration and perhaps the most important for liaisons to understand as we move into the future. Making determinations as to which databases should be added and which dropped can vary considerably as well across institutions. In rare cases, a college or university may need to subscribe directly to a given resource. In most cases, however, databases are accessed through consortial arrangements. A library pools its money with other relevant libraries in order to receive better pricing from a vendor. For example, in North Carolina, NC LIVE bundles together a number of subscriptions, giving patrons in North Carolina libraries access to more resources than they might otherwise have if each library stood alone. According to its website, "NC LIVE is North Carolina's statewide online library service. Founded in 1997 by representatives from the NC Community Colleges, the NC Independent Colleges and Universities, the NC Public Library Directors Association, the University of North Carolina and the State Library of North Carolina . . . [it] serves nearly 200 member libraries across North Carolina."[10] Through NC LIVE, as with other consortia, libraries pool their funds in order to provide more online resources to patrons "that support education, enhance statewide economic development, and increase quality of life."[11] In Rhode Island, the Higher Education Library Network provides institutions of higher education a similar opportunity for collective bargaining with vendors.[12] As you might surmise, saving money on these subscriptions comes with a price of a different kind. While liaisons might prefer access to specific databases, they might also need to consider the compromises made across not just campuses but institutions as well. As with periodicals, they might additionally consider the implications regarding the ongoing cost for access to a resource. It is often not without potential negative repercussions. If faculty and students get comfortable with a resource only to have it removed the following year, this can create dissatisfaction with services. As stated, knowledge of databases and database selection is an absolutely critical area for any liaison as more and more resources move toward online availability.

Library liaisons must also consider the collection balance from print to electronic. This is an area of change that has been evident for a very long time. For example, e-books in academic libraries have exploded from 64.3 million in 2006 to 158.7 million in 2010.[13] Likewise, academic library spending for electronic serial subscriptions has also exploded from $691.6 million in 2006 to $1.2 billion in 2010.[14] The electronic trend seems to be continuing to accelerate. One of the big issues arising from this is that each of these areas of resources (print versus electronic) cannot always be managed in isolation. For example, each time the database bill increases, this may negatively impact a library's ability to purchase print resources. Sometimes an institution can provide additional funding for the library, but more commonly the library will be asked to make internal allocations work without additional overall funds. According to Ellen McNair, "perhaps funds are not available to purchase the same number of books at the same rate we have in the past and increase the digital resources students need to transition into a global, digital workforce."[15] She states, "Knowing that fewer print books will be purchased increases the significance of our choices."[16] These decisions are not usually easy and require great diligence on the part of the library liaison.

Liaisons' involvement in the acquisitions process will typically require a balance of print and electronic spending. With the increasing demand for e-books and the cost of electronic materials, it is challenging to balance these costs with other library resources. Included in these challenges are an understanding of consortia and the advantages and disadvantages of group buying. Additionally, liaisons must understand the purchasing process for both one-time and ongoing materials. Acquisitions reflect the logistical aspect of collection development once items have been selected.

Acquisitions Checklist

☐ One-time purchase methods
☐ Ongoing periodical purchases
☐ Database selection and consortia
☐ Balancing print versus electronic resources

Budgeting

The budgeting process for most libraries in recent years has been a painful one. As we seek to enhance resources and services, the economic downturn and the public outcry for greater accountability for institutions of higher education have led to the need to justify all expenses to a more significant degree than historically required. In the past, when libraries were seen as warehouses of knowledge and access to interlibrary loan services and online resources was more limited, libraries were often funded so that they could comprehensively collect in any number of areas. The library landscape has changed dramatically in the past two decades. Libraries now must be accountable for their spending and utilize all methods available to access resources.

In recent years, libraries have been forced to emphasize access over ownership at a rapid pace. This has not been without its rewards. The more integrated role of the library liaison and other library staff as teachers with regard to information literacy is no doubt exciting. However, the relevance of the library as a result of recent developments has become more nebulous from the perspective of the public and the academic community. It is often no longer necessary even to go to the library to access a wide variety of databases. This sometimes makes administrators question the value of the library and its physical collections. Aside from advocating for the library itself and all of its elements and services, the liaison can play a critical role in establishing and maintaining an adequate library budget. When the library budget is constructed, the liaison is the single most knowledgeable person to speak to the needs in a given area and from his or her unique perspective.

The process of budgeting can vary across institutions. It is necessary to understand the history of budgeting at a given institution and any political ramifications associated with it. For some libraries, the library committee may determine how funds for collection development are allocated. In other libraries, a specific formula might be applied and carried from one year to the next. For example, at the G. A. Pfeiffer Library at Pfeiffer University in Charlotte, the book budget is determined by departmental enrollment, credit hours taught, and majors offered at the junior and senior levels.[17] At Austin Peay State University's Felix G. Woodward Library, funds are determined by four factors: flat base per department, student credit hours (weighted freshman year through graduate level), publishing volume of the discipline, and average price of book per discipline.[18] Still other libraries have experimented with connecting funds to the budgets of specific program areas. One creative approach in recent years has been the use of the balanced score card (BSC). The BSC concept emerged from the business world. In a nutshell, this budgeting process requires the library to squeeze from operating expenses funds that can then be strategically utilized in addressing a future need. For example, the University of Virginia's library is one that utilizes the BSC. This approach forces the library liaisons and other library staff to focus on outcomes that are most important for key stakeholders.[19] Budgeting can be challenging, but it also always provides this opportunity to explore what the real value of the library is at a given institution and where the library liaison in particular can have the greatest impact.

In order to decide on collection purchases, liaisons must be aware of the budget allocation methods in place at their respective institutions. As these methods determine how funds are spent, it is critical information for a librarian trying to enhance a subject-specific collection area. As budget dollars are stretched, liaisons reach out for information access through consortium buying power as well as interlibrary loans.

Budgeting Checklist

☐ Spending accountability
☐ Access versus ownership of materials
☐ Budget allocation methods

Conclusion

Library liaisons must be familiar with an institution's collection development policy and insert themselves into the process of constantly reviewing and adapting this document as necessary. Liaisons must be open to and actively seek suggestions on a regular basis and must also be familiar with a library's process of handling specific requests for materials and resources. They must play a role in determining how the library's collections will be assessed and must spend time considering the results of such assessments and implications for the future. Library liaisons must also have an understanding of the acquisitions process for both print and electronic materials. Last, liaison librarians must understand the budgeting process at their college or university and positively influence discussions, always with the idea of better serving critical constituencies.

NOTES

1. Fred J. Hay, "Subject Specialist in the Academic Library: A Review Article," *Journal of Academic Librarianship* 16, no. 1 (1990): 12.

2. Harvard Law School Library, "Harvard Law School Library Mission," *Harvard University*, www.law.harvard.edu/library/about/mission/index.html.

3. Harvard Law School Library, "Collection Development Country List," *Harvard University*, www.law.harvard.edu/library/about/collections/index.html.

4. Association of Research Libraries, "ARL Statistics and Salary Surveys," www.arl.org/focus-areas/statistics-assessment/arl-statistics-salary-survey.

5. Ibid.

6. YBP Library Services, "U.S. Core Titles," *Baker & Taylor*, www.ybp.com/acad/core1000cover.htm.

7. OCLC, "WorldCat Collection Analysis," *Online Computer Library Center, Inc.*, www.oclc.org/collectionanalysis/.

8. Lydia Knight, "Encouraging Faculty Requests for Library Materials: Midwest's New Book Selection Service," *Georgia Library Quarterly* 46, no. 3 (2009): 12–13.

9. "Your Total E-resource Management System: EBSCONET," *EBSCO*, www2.ebsco.com/en-us/ProductsServices/ebsconet/Pages/index.aspx.

10. NC LIVE, "NC LIVE: About," *NCLIVE.org*, www.nclive.org/about.

11. Ibid.

12. "HELIN: About HELIN: Mission and Goals," *HELIN Library Consortium, Inc.*, www.helininc.org/General/mission.html.

13. Denise M. Davis, "The Condition of U.S. Libraries: Academic Library Trends, 1999–2009," *ALA Office of Research and Statistics*, www.ala.org/research/sites/ala.org.research/files/content/librarystats/academic/Condition_of_Libraries_1999.20.pdf: 16; United States Department of Education, "Academic Libraries: 2010 First Look," *Institute of Education Sciences*, http://nces.ed.gov/pubs2012/2012365.pdf:2.

14. Davis, "The Condition of U.S. Libraries," 12; United States Department of Education, "Academic Libraries: 2010," 2.

15. Ellen McNair, "Print to Digital: Opportunities for Choice," *Library Media Connection* 30, no. 6 (2012): 28.

16. Ibid.

17. John A. Mercer, "Budget Allocation Formulas" [mailing list archives], *COLLDV-L*, http://serials.infomotions.com/colldv-l/archive/2010/201002/0028.html.

18. Elizabeth Futas, ed., "Budget Book Allocation Formula," in *Library Acquisition Policies and Procedures*, 2nd ed. (Phoenix, AZ: Oryx, 1984), http://library.apsu.edu/library/3_6formula.htm.

19. Michele M. Reid, "Is the Balanced Scorecard Right for Academic Libraries?," *The Bottom Line: Managing Library Finances* 24, no. 2 (2011): 85–95; University of Virginia, "UVa Balanced Scorecard Improves Collection Management," *BSC Designer*, www.bscdesigner.com/uva-library-balanced-scorecard-improves-collection-management.htm.

Teaching Information Literacy

As a liaison librarian, the task of teaching a library instruction session that incorporates information literacy standards will often be expected and can be a large component of the faculty assistance liaisons provide in some institutions. It can be a common experience for liaisons new to their job in an academic library to be confronted with the challenge of teaching despite limited skills and experience in this area. As stated in the article "Dangerous Liaisons? Defining the Faculty Liaison Librarian Service Model, Its Effectiveness and Sustainability,"

> The complexity of the information environment has, however, allowed
> liaison librarians to grasp the function of information literacy as one of
> the ways to re-integrate themselves with the faculties and their clients.
> Many academic libraries have promoted this educative task as the major
> part of the liaison librarians' job.[1]

This ability to "re-integrate" reinforces the importance of information literacy in the academic library. Often, the librarian will not have any formal teaching experience or training and will perhaps be nervous about speaking in front of a class. Some liaisons may have some difficulty understanding what is required in the information literacy instruction. In fact, even the term *information literacy*, which is a standards-based skill used as a foundation for library instruction learning outcomes, is not deeply understood by many new librarians. With these ideas in mind, it is pertinent to explore information literacy and understand how it forms the foundation of academic library instruction. This knowledge can help answer the questions "What do I do now?" and "How do I teach?" when teaching a class presents itself to a library liaison.

Information Literacy

How is information literacy defined? The Association of College and Research Libraries formally defined the principal tenets in 2000.[2] ACRL defined the information-literate individual as one who has gained an understanding of the nature and extent of the need for information, understands how to access and evaluate information, and presents it in a responsible manner. Certainly, there are more facets and related concepts associated with the term *information literacy*, and it is not so easy to assess an individual's information literacy skill set. However, having a basic understanding of information literacy is a good starting point for approaching library instruction. The majority of higher education libraries with library instruction programs use information literacy concepts and standards as a template for building their classes. Therefore, it can be advantageous to become familiar with the concept and its implications. As expected, the information provided by ACRL is a great source for information literacy assistance. On its targeted website (www .ala.org/acrl/issues/infolit), ACRL provides a starting point with overviews, resources, guides, and programs if a greater understanding of information literacy is needed.[3] The ACRL's Immersion Program is a worthwhile endeavor if there is interest in improving library instruction skills (www.ala.org/acrl/ immersionprogram).

To expand upon the abbreviated definition above, the five ACRL standards that compose information literacy are listed here:

Standard One: The information literate student determines the nature and extent of the information needed.

Standard Two: The information literate student accesses needed information effectively and efficiently.

Standard Three: The information literate student evaluates information and its sources critically and incorporates selected information into his or her knowledge base and value system.

Standard Four: The information literate student, individually or as a member of a group, uses information effectively to accomplish a specific purpose.

Standard Five: The information literate student understands many of the economic, legal, and social issues surrounding the use of information and accesses and uses information ethically and legally.[4]

These underlying tenets of information literacy do not need to be explicitly expressed to students in most basic library instruction classes. The concepts as they are written may actually confuse student expectations about the material and how the standards are part of a class in the library. An important consideration is that, for some students, the class may be their first in a library. Despite the fact that the words *information literacy* may never be uttered in the class, having an awareness of the ways in which information literacy is a bedrock of library instruction can affect the way in which students are taught.

It is important to keep in mind that the liaison role and the teaching of information literacy combine to form a bridge to both faculty and students. Information literacy continues to grow as an integral aspect of librarianship. Once the foundational concepts of information literacy are understood and then embedded in library instruction by the liaison, one contribution to the student is awareness that high-quality research is dependent on the quality of resources. This can then improve the quality of the paper, which in turn is appreciated by the teacher. If the library liaison is able to get students to understand the value of improving their research skill set and additionally gain confidence in their own ability to do research, this adds to their employability and their lifelong learning. Furthermore, the students' concept of what a librarian can do for them, and thus the value of their academic library, is enhanced.

The liaison role in reference to information literacy also helps to formulate a more modern concept of the library. For students, the library becomes a place that supersedes its former perceived role as an information warehouse to become an environment where knowledge is created. Therefore, a concept inherent in the liaison role of library instructor is promoting to students and faculty a new perspective on the library that is formulated around the concept of a relationship with librarians and information. Debra Gilchrist and Megan Oakleaf crystallize the importance of information literacy. They make the following observation:

> To be prepared for academic study, life, and work, students must become critical consumers and users of information. Inherent in the construct of information literacy is the recognition of inquiry as central to learning as well as fluency with the systems and strategies that facilitate that quest.[5]

In summation, the liaison librarian needs to have an awareness of information literacy and the role it plays in the library and throughout the institution. Understanding this concept and how it affects student development and reliance on librarians can help to improve how the liaison presents library instruction. By no means does this introduction cover all aspects of information literacy, yet it offers a handoff to the liaison for learning more.

Information Literacy Basics Checklist

☐ IL defined and ACRL standards
☐ Understanding IL learning standards
☐ Lifelong value of IL

Instruction Basics

Now that the basic information literacy concepts have been defined, it would seem that the general idea of how to conduct library instruction with twenty-five or thirty English composition students would be clearer. Yet library instruction is not quite that easy or clear-cut. The content that is covered can vary greatly based on the needs of the students. If given the opportunity, a liaison's best course of action, after gaining some basic understanding of information literacy, is to take some time to observe library instruction sessions taught by fellow librarians before taking a turn at one. If needed, library liaisons can look to other university or college libraries in the local area and ask to sit in on one of their sessions. This can be worthwhile for a number of reasons. The most obvious is to gain an understanding of what content and format library instruction can entail. Another plus is that a relationship can form with the library instructor and thus mentorship possibilities may evolve. Finally, information literacy session observations may boost confidence in personal abilities because concepts such as presentation pace and time management are regularly incorporated. Observation of information literacy being taught by experienced librarians is the first step in becoming an IL teacher.

When preparing for an information literacy session, preplanning is a must. There can be many variables related to the scheduling of the session itself, such as whether the school is on semesters or terms, where the class is being taught, and how the faculty member schedules the class. Depending on staff size and instruction volume, some institutions have one librarian who handles the scheduling and teaching of classes, while others have library instruction coordinators who plan out the teaching schedules for a number of instruction librarians or subject specialists. Once the presentation time, meeting place, and other scheduling details have been decided, an effort should be made to contact the instructor of the class. Ideally, one should attempt to meet with the faculty member in person well in advance. As indicated in chapter 3, the foundation for a relationship and communication should already be in place. If the professor is new or a relationship has not been established, send an e-mail of introduction as the librarian who will be teaching the class. This correspondence should determine the most current, required class assignment and the goals of the information literacy session. Is the session a basic IL introduction, evaluation of resources, or a specifically tailored presentation? Once the parameters are determined, the library liaison should give the professor a brief synopsis of what is planned for the presentation to the students. These are very important liaison steps when preparing for IL instruction. The ability to communicate well with faculty will facilitate a better presentation and build a better reputation for future liaison activities.

Once introductions and logistics are completed for the information literacy session, perhaps the most important thing to keep in mind is the need to tie in the IL content with an assignment the class is currently working on. It can be extremely difficult to engage students and keep their interest if they do not see relevant value in the presentation of library resources. Understanding the research requirements of the assignment allows the IL session to be tailored to student need. The session should reflect which resources are most optimal for the students to use. For example, if a freshman English class has been given an assignment to write a paper on the topic of sustainability, a database such as EBSCONhost's GreenFILE or Gale's GREENR could be presented, with extra attention given to showing the ease of citing an article from within the database. Students respond best when they watch a session where the research part of the assignment is taken, a sample topic is created, and appropriate resources are presented. An approach might be along the lines of "This is how the librarian would perform college-level research on sustainability" with an emphasis on current journal articles, thereby supporting ACRL Standard Three. A previous understanding of the assignment requirements and mentioning these as well as showing how students can meet them are excellent ways to sustain the students' attention. Through such steps, the information literacy session is linked to a relevant classroom assignment and becomes meaningful to students.

While there are by no means set templates for what a library instruction session looks like or the content it covers, some general topics can be presented. This content could include the following:

- Accessing and navigating the OPAC to find library materials
- Locating library materials (physically by classification location and virtually) once they are found in the OPAC
- Choosing specific databases and how to access them
- Reviewing the design of a specific database and how to choose the options within it
- Narrowing or broadening a database results list
- Noting citation tools available within a database
- Narrowing or choosing the topic
- Determining valid supporting materials (facts, statistics, quotes)
- Evaluating information and resources

A quick glance at this list might reveal that there is a gap in one's own comprehensive knowledge of library resources or even perhaps citation style and format. It would not leave a favorable impression to make a presentation as a library liaison to students and faculty, but be unable to demonstrate how to navigate a specific database. Therefore, it is important for the liaison to take some time to get to know as much as possible about the resources that the library extends to students. A library liaison has a responsibility to have a deep understanding of the material that is being taught. Again, confidence is a key and the benefits of learning the structure and features of the databases the library has to offer are manifold.

Considering the design of the information literacy sessions in relation to the ACRL standards, all of the standards can be touched on in library instruction, but here only two will be discussed in depth. When it comes to ACRL Standard Three specifically, evaluating resources, perhaps some thought can be made to determine what type of presentation best fits this standard. One consideration here is that the idea of evaluation ties in nicely with some of the basic tenets of scientific inquiry. Being skeptical about information helps one to evaluate it. It can be helpful for students to see how this line of thought parallels with science and the need to be skeptical when evaluating information. Pointing out the relevance and value of evaluating practical information is also a good practice. Students then may be wary or skeptical of what they read and evaluate the information put before them when signing a contract for a car or an apartment lease. These examples can resonate more immediately with students and translate to evaluating a suspect website and thereby achieving better research resources. In contrast to the "real-world" implications of evaluating information, in teaching to an English class that is focused more on ACRL Standard One (determining what information is needed), some students may drift and have a hard time grasping the value of this third standard or feel intimidated about the tools being shown. They may also feel as though the difficulty and unfamiliarity of the database's design is too large of a hurdle to overcome, especially in comparison to search engines such as Google, with which they are typically more familiar. When teaching ACRL Standard Three, a good tactic is providing a bridge to concrete day-to-day examples that may not be tied to an academic assignment. Criteria such as accuracy, authority, currency, objectivity, and relevance can be used as evaluation markers to show students how to measure the validity of information for daily life and in class assignments.

The concept of the need to evaluate sources is relatively easy to grasp. Having some type of criteria to measure information helps students understand this standard a bit more easily. This can also be the most rewarding type of library instruction to perform. Students are often reluctant to change their search strategies or move to unfamiliar information sources, but they find that evaluating information is a good idea and can affect them in everyday information transactions. Providing examples of how their daily lives are impacted by poor information choices often drives home the point. It can be eye-opening for a student to realize that a financial decision based on poor information can translate into a bad purchase or that researching a medical condition using unreliable information from a website can have far-reaching health consequences.

Whether it is the first or the hundredth library instruction session, the liaison should have an awareness of the basic preparation needed and produce content that creates the most worth for students. An understanding of the ACRL standards is the foundation for all information literacy instruction, and mapping them to learning outcomes and content helps to create value. Liaisons should preplan IL presentations and research current class assignments to create a presentation that is meaningful to students. Engaging students so that they benefit in their research creates value for them and value for the liaison librarian.

Teaching Basics Checklist

☐ IL session observation
☐ Preplanning logistics
☐ Class assignment tie-in
☐ General IL content
☐ Evaluating information resources

Learning Outcomes and Assessment

Once an understanding of information literacy terminology and concepts is gained and time is allotted to prepare for the library instruction, the next step is to determine some learning outcomes for the students. Learning outcomes can be summed up as "statements that describe what students should be able to demonstrate" when they have completed a course, program, or other learning experience.[6] These outcomes express abstract concepts and skill sets.[7] It is imperative to consider what research tools and skills the students are taking with them when they exit the IL session. This can be difficult to ascertain and may take some time or a number of sessions to gauge. In addition to helping formulate learning outcomes, understanding students' range of research skills and their knowledge of the research process is also related to assessment, which will be covered later in this chapter. An important factor when assessing a student is the time that assessment will take place. Students can be assessed for their knowledge of library resources and research strategies and skills before, during, or after a library instruction session, as well as a combination of these three.

Depending on many variables, the number of learning outcomes can be a short or long list. Perhaps the first thing to consider is the length of the class time. Taking the generic fifty-minute session as a default, three learning outcomes can be considered an appropriate number. It is important to remember that the students have numerous duties themselves, including other classes, potentially work or career responsibilities, and other obligations. It is therefore recommended that one consider the idea that less can be more. Also note that students can retain only a small amount of all of the resources, tips, and information that are relayed to them. As James Thull and Mary Anne Hansen describe it,

> Librarians can be so eager to share their knowledge of the library resources available to students that they can simply overwhelm them. Being interactive and using humor can go a long way towards creating a comfortable atmosphere and helping the students remember the librarian and hopefully some of what they learned about the library and its resources.[8]

Constructing learning outcomes can be a difficult exercise. One tip that may help is to use the phrase *in order to* (as used in the examples below) as a connector between the content being presented and the skill set desired for students. Therefore, these three learning outcomes exercises are offered as examples:

Work through some search strategies and examples that display valuable information results in order to initiate and promote students' confidence in their information-seeking capabilities.

Discuss the impact of good and bad information results in order to recognize the value of quality information-seeking skills.

Define and experiment with library resources in order to bolster students' ability to fulfill academic information needs.

Even if learning outcomes are not presented in writing to the class, communicated to students, or reviewed when teaching, it is a good idea to think about what needs to be imparted to students. Because a liaison librarian may be new to librarianship, it can initially be overwhelming to think about pedagogy. However, as liaisons become adjusted to teaching information literacy, the desire for improvement will push into directions of examining teaching styles and skills. An engaged liaison librarian will be researching learning styles and active learning strategies, and trying to find a personal voice as a librarian teacher. Once this is accomplished and the material is familiar, the liaison is well on the way to becoming an essential asset to the library and fulfilling the role as a valued information literacy instructor.

The ACRL standards should be embedded within the learning outcomes. The first standard (determining the nature and extent of information needed) can be especially overlooked. A good liaison should understand when students require help identifying their need for information. The critical concept here revolves around the word *information* and one's relationship to it. Certainly it is beyond the scope of this chapter, much less this book, to address all of the meaning and implied ideas inherent in the concept of information and one's relationship to it. Suffice to say, volumes have been written on the subject. For our purposes, here the principal idea is that students may not have an awareness of the research process and some of the information assets that the library provides. For example, students may not be aware that library databases contain articles that may be more reliable and authoritative than those they might come across in a Google search. In fact, students may not be aware that there are academic journal articles available to them in a library database. Taking it a step further, some students may not even understand what is meant by the term *database*. As a liaison who may be required to teach in a number of library instruction sessions, the instructional librarian now has the responsibility to consider the students and their relationship to information. Through good and informative IL sessions, the liaison can provide this needed research support to the students.

Assessment can include feedback on how well the instructional librarian is doing in the presentations. When assessing and attempting to discover if the goals created are actually being achieved, the results can help to further development as a teaching librarian. Assessment data is also used by many academic libraries to show the value of the instruction program, the librarians, and the library itself. This topic is covered extensively in chapter 11. Because of the value of feedback, it is easy to see why it is important to plan out and create assessment tools for library instruction. Considering the goals and measuring if they are being fulfilled is a core principle of library instruction. Without learning outcomes and assessment, library instruction could be seen as an empty and meaningless practice or one in which errors are repeated. The constant need to reflect and evaluate on what is being done separates achievement from rote exercise. A good resource for exploring learning outcomes is Teresa Y. Neely's *Information Literacy Assessment: Standards-Based Tools and Assignments.*[9]

Underlying all IL sessions should be basic learning outcomes. While not openly expressed to the students, the library liaison should have an awareness of these goals when creating the information literacy presentations or workshops. When weaving these outcomes into the material to be learned, liaisons should not assume students have an understanding of basic terms or research methods. Assessing their level of understanding is a component of IL instruction in order to advance their skills. Information literacy instruction, like all education, must be based on defined learning outcomes and continually assessed to support the library liaison as teaching librarian.

Learning Outcomes Checklist

- ☐ Baseline of knowledge
- ☐ Outcomes defined
- ☐ Creating learning outcomes
- ☐ Assessing learning

Format, Pedagogy, and Other Considerations

It can be difficult to include all academic library environments when discussing in general terms how a library instruction session is defined. Many instruction librarians use terms like "one-shot" and "fifty-minute session" to describe traditional information literacy sessions. This is where the allotted presentation time is fifty minutes and there is just one meeting (as opposed to a semester-long class) to impress upon students how to conduct research. There are alternatives to this type of library instruction. Many libraries are moving their instruction online and there have been cases showing how a well-constructed online IL session improves student learning.[10] Additionally, many academic libraries have graduated from numerous shorter sessions and have constructed semester-long information literacy courses for credit. There are credit-bearing information literacy courses being taught at a number of institutions, and books such as C. V. Hollister's *Best Practices for Credit-Bearing Information Literacy Courses* can help with their design.[11]

Within these various instructional formats there is a growing desire to teach information use and critical thinking skills. Additionally, students may not have access to such items as library databases in their future careers.

Because of these factors, library instruction should be more than simply "point and click shows" that merely offer an overview of library resources. If the liaison has an opportunity for more than simply a one-shot IL session, there are a number of other areas on which to focus IL skills. One of these areas is evaluation of resources, as mentioned earlier. Another is topic-specific presentations as coordinated with the professor. Teaching students the importance of developing their basic ability to find information, whether by using a library database or a search engine, should take precedence over the types of sources shown during library instruction. Often, it is a good idea to stress the value to students of gaining research skills and how that can affect their employability and lifelong learning.

In addition to format, the IL presentation setting is another consideration. The manner in which the material is taught can also be affected by the design of the classroom or computer lab that is available, and there are a myriad of setups that may be encountered. Students can be seated in rows, grouped together, in a circle, or perhaps in modular, movable desks. Does the setting promote student interactions with one another? Is there an area for white-board (or paper) usage by the students as part of the class? One of the most common current configurations is a lab where the library liaison stands at a podium with a computer connected to a projector while a number of students, each with his or her own desktop computer, follow along. The library liaison should also evaluate the technology available beforehand. This influences the way in which information can be presented. It is often a good idea to practice an instructional session in advance. Using the actual presentation room (if possible) is a plus. This allows for the liaison librarian to gain an understanding of the technology to be used and increases confidence and the level of comfort before presenting. Will the students have their own computers? Is a presentation screen and projector available? Can the presenter control and monitor student computers? Just as with orientation meeting presentations, it is also wise to have nontechnical options in case something goes wrong with expected technology (for example, loss of access to a specific database). As wish many endeavors, the more planning that takes place before a library instructional session, the better the presentation will be, and evaluating the setting is part of this process.

Pedagogy, or the method of teaching, is another consideration for IL instructors. Often, any former teaching or training experience is the first light that guides the library liaison when placed in front of a room of students.

Emulating a favorite teacher's style may also influence the teaching method. Pedagogical style can even be a matter of beginning library instruction by using the same tools that a trainer or mentor uses. Currently, presentation software may be Microsoft PowerPoint or Prezi. Presentation software may alternatively be dispensed with altogether, and the instruction could begin by jumping right to the library website to show students how to access library and other information resources. The key here for liaisons is taking some time to find the most comfortable presentation style and continue to improve on it.

Studies have shown that active learning can be a very effective pedagogical tactic.[12] The ability to move away from lecturing to spending the majority of the time involved with a hands-on element for the students can create a well-paced, engaging learning environment. It can also be a benefit for the instructor when managing time. Using a mix of short bursts of lecturing and information with some hands-on activities for students can improve attention. Another approach is to get students involved from the very beginning of the class by prompting them with questions and discussion points. As mentioned previously, it can take time, practice, and preparation to become comfortable with a method of teaching. An excellent way to explore different learning styles and ways in which to address them is to review different exercises that have already been created. Joanna M. Burkhardt and Mary C. MacDonald's book *Teaching Information Literacy; 50 Standards-Based Exercises for College Students*, now in its second edition, is a good resource for this.[13]

Library liaisons should be aware that students may not be prepared for the specific content that information literacy sessions are intending to cover, and they may feel unsure about using library services. The students may need a solid introduction to the material presented. A good beginning approach is to start IL sessions by welcoming students to the library. If the presentation is being taught outside the library, still initiate the class with a welcoming, warm tone. After an introduction, an overview of the basic points to be covered and relaying the learning goals early on in the presentation can be the next steps. Often asking questions about how many have been to the library or used databases before can help determine existing knowledge. Anxiety is a well-documented emotion that students who are unfamiliar with the library often have of both the library and librarians.[14] A 2006 study by Joel Battle at Texas Women's University compared library anxiety among students before and after a fourteen-week information literacy course.[15] After the course, students felt significantly more comfortable with using the library and its resources.[16]

In addition to IL content, the library liaison should also pay careful attention to the image that is projected to students. As a speaker, the liaison should neatly dress one level above the students' attire, and if a female presenter, be conservative with jewelry and makeup.[17] Both body language and tone of voice impact delivery. The best approach is to simply have a conversation with the audience.[18] Moving away from the podium, facing the students, and using gestures are all recommended for a better presentation.[19] While the liaison wants to project a knowledgeable and authoritative image, he or she also wants to be approachable. If the library liaison is open and conveys a desire to help, the IL session will be a success from the perspective of creating a future conduit to students. Students will remember that the librarian is there to assist them with their research needs and is willing to create an environment of mutual respect. When library instruction is taught, it effectively is "encouraging patrons to use the academic materials that the libraries acquire to support their disciplines."[20]

Information literacy instruction can be delivered in one-shot sessions, over the course of a semester, or even as a credit course. Liaison librarians must adjust and plan accordingly for the amount of time available with students. The presentation space, format, and instructional style should be determined in advance. Active learning will engage and interest students.[21] Additionally, an awareness of student anxiety with the often unfamiliar resources and services the library offers should influence the method and content of the presentation. When taking a sweeping view of the information literacy presentation, liaisons should remember to keep it simple and relevant.

Format and Pedagogy Checklist

☐ One-shot, semester-long, or credit course
☐ Presentation format and setting
☐ Pedagogy
☐ Active learning and student anxiety

Conclusion

Because a primary goal of the liaison is to promote the library's resources and services, information literacy and library instruction play a crucial role. For review, these steps can help with information literacy instruction and reinforce the liaison's bridge to students and faculty. First, take some time to become familiar with the core elements of information literacy, particularly the standards provided by the ACRL. Second, observe fellow instruction librarians to gain confidence. Third, prepare for a library instruction session by contacting the instructor of the class and asking about the current assignment students are working on. Develop a presentation relevant to the research. Next, practice in the classroom and use the available technology. (Be sure to vary the instruction with lecture, discussion, and hands-on activities.) Finally, use the standards as a foundation for the learning outcomes students should gain once they have completed the IL session. With preparation, planning, and practice, information literacy instruction will be a success!

NOTES

1. John Rodwell and Linden Fairbairn, "Dangerous Liaisons? Defining the Faculty Liaison Librarian Service Model, Its Effectiveness and Sustainability," *Library Management* 29, no. 1–2 (2008): 120.

2. "Information Literacy Competency Standards for Higher Education," *Association of College & Research Libraries*, www.ala.org/acrl/standards/informationliteracy competency#ildef.

3. Ibid.

4. Ibid.

5. Debra Gilchrist and Megan Oakleaf, "An Essential Partner: The Librarian's Role in Student Learning Assessment," Occasional Paper #14, *National Institute for Learning Outcomes Assessment*, www.learningoutcomeassessment.org/documents/ LibraryLO_000.pdf: 4.

6. Peter Hernon, "What Really Are Student Learning Outcomes?" (presentation), American Library Association National Conference, Seattle, Washington, March 12–15, 2009, www.ala.org/acrl/sites/ala.org.acrl/files/content/conferences/confsand preconfs/national/seattle/papers/28.pdf: 30.

7. Ibid.

8. James Thull and Mary Anne Hansen, "Academic Library Liaison Programs in U.S. Libraries: Methods and Benefits," *New Library World* 110, no. 11 (2009): 533.

9. Teresa Y. Neely, *Information Literacy Assessment: Standards-Based Tools and Assignments* (Chicago: American Library Association, 2006).

10. Glenda A. Gunter, "The Effects of the Impact of Instructional Immediacy on Cognition and Learning in Online Classes," *International Journal of Social Sciences* 2, no. 3 (2007): 195.

11. Christopher Vance Hollister, ed., *Best Practices for Credit-Bearing Information Literacy Courses* (Chicago: Association of College and Research Libraries, 2010).

12. Co Fata-Hartley, "Resisting Rote: The Importance of Active Learning for All Course Learning Objectives," *Journal of College Science Teaching* 40, no. 3 (2011): 36.

13. Jeanna M. Burkhardt and Mary C. MacDonald, with Andrée J. Rathemacher, *Teaching Information Literacy: 50 Standards-Based Exercises for College Students,* 2nd ed. (Chicago: ALA Editions, 2010).

14. Qun G. Jiao and Anthony J. Onwuegbuzie, "Self-Perception and Library Anxiety: An Empirical Study," *Library Review* 48, no. 3 (1999): 141.

15. Joel Battle, "Information Literacy Instruction for Educators and the Role of School and Academic Libraries," *Texas Library Journal* 83, no. 3 (2007): 121.

16. Ibid., 125.

17. T. J. Walker, *How to Give a Pretty Good Presentation* (Hoboken, NJ: John Wiley and Sons, 2010), 40.

18. Lenny Laskowski, *Painless Presentations: The Proven, Stress-Free Way to Successful Public Speaking* (Hoboken, NJ: John Wiley and Sons, 2012), 131.

19. Ibid., 126–27.

20. Thull and Hansen, "Academic Library Liaison Programs," 532.

21. Samina Malik and Fouzia Janjua, "Active Lecturing: An Effective Pedagogic Approach," *International Journal of Academic Research* 3, no. 2 (2011): 963.

Embedded Librarianship

Library liaisons are increasingly expected to play the role of an embedded librarian. What exactly does it mean to be an embedded librarian? Put simply, an embedded librarian is one who is assisting with information services at the point of need with students and faculty.[1] These embedded librarians provide many of the traditional liaison services, but in unique and deeply connected ways. David Shumaker addresses this distinction by pointing out that the embedded "librarian becomes a member of the customer community rather than a service provider standing apart."[2] In creating an effective embedded liaison program, Shumaker and Mary Talley offer a five-step system. These steps are building relationships, learning the organization and subject, offering valued services, building alliances, and securing managerial support.[3] Work as an embedded librarian is often a job unto itself. Instead of waiting idly by a reference desk for students to approach, the embedded librarian ventures into student spaces and often becomes an instructional partner to the main professor. Embedded liaison work takes a proactive librarian who will plan, initiate, and carry out the many duties it encompasses.

As a library liaison, the connection made with faculty and students lends itself perfectly to establishing an embedded presence. It is through the established relationship with a faculty member that an embedded librarian will

> **Library liaison.** A librarian located in the library assisting through liaison support and services. This librarian is an agent of communication.
>
> **Embedded librarian.** A librarian located online, in the classroom, or in a department assisting with liaison support and services. This librarian communicates as part of the group.

have access to both information and students in order to assist with information literacy and research needs. Librarians embed themselves in classes, in different physical spaces on campus, and in virtual spaces. As alluded to throughout this book, collaboration and relationships are at the core of being a successful liaison. A strong working relationship with assigned faculty members increases the chance of embedment in the class. Once again the personal connection with faculty and students will be a critical element in making an embedded liaison successful whether contact is virtual or in person.

The embedded librarian must work with the class professor in order to deliver his or her services. Collaboration is a must. The faculty instructor holds the key to the classroom door. Without this liaison-faculty relationship, embedded librarianship cannot exist. At times the librarian may be involved on the front end of a course and help with its initial development. When classes begin, an embedded librarian may explore the course syllabus and readings with the instructor. From this, the liaison should develop awareness of course requirements and grading expectations of the professor with class research projects. This enables the library liaison to form a parallel outlook of course objectives and outcomes with the instructor. As the course continues, information literacy instruction and other research services can be integrated. Assistance with writing class assignments may also take place in order to incorporate information literacy and research skills. After the class has concluded, feedback can be used by both the embedded librarian and faculty member to improve the learning environment for next time. If it sounds like the embedded librarian is approaching a coteaching position, this may be a realistic analysis. Library liaisons who are embedded are assisting with student learning.

Before further exploring the embedded librarian world of today, it is good to know how the concept came to be a component of liaison work. While the terminology *embedded librarian* was first used in 2004, the roots of this concept began much earlier.[4] It was in the early 1990s with the introduction of CD-ROMs and online resources that roving reference began to take place and librarians began to seek out users at their point of need.[5] This concept led librarians to experiment with placement in a number of nonlibrary locations, such as student unions, dorms, and other outposts, trying to connect to the user.[6] While many of those experiments failed, librarians did discover their presence in academic departments and classes made a difference. This was a perfect connection for the library liaison assigned to a specific subject area of the college or university. As a result, today's embedded librarian is now connected in three areas—online classes, in-person classes, and within a department of the college or university. Embedment has become a growing function of liaison work.

Online Embedment

One of the most common forms of embedment is through online learning or course management software. In order for a library liaison to be embedded online, access to such software (for example, Moodle, Sakai, or Blackboard) is the first step. Communication with the class instructor as well as the information technology department may be necessary to accomplish this setup. Access may require the library liaison to be entered into the courseware as a student, coteacher, or guest lecturer.[7] If this is not possible, embedding library liaison communication links or a chat option on the class page may be another alternative.[8] Sometimes the embedded librarian becomes a type of coteacher in an online class and is given full access by the instructor to the online learning management software class. Each learning software system uses a different name for this type of embedment.

Being incorporated into the software pages of the online class will enable the librarian to do more for the students. Once there, what exactly does an online embedded librarian do? John Shank and Nancy Dewald helped define embedded librarian online activities in a 2003 article for *Information Technology and Libraries.* (The Library and Information Technology

Association, which publishes this journal, is a division of the ALA.) They listed the areas of embedded liaison service as follows:

1. Delivering library instruction online
2. Providing research guides
3. Recommending databases
4. Posting reference style sheets (APA, MLA)
5. Assisting with reference (e-mail, chat, discussion board)
6. Embedding tutorials
7. Utilizing quizzes (pre- and posttesting of IL instruction)
8. Soliciting feedback through questionnaires[9]

Shank, along with Steven Bell, updated these roles in a 2011 article introducing the concept of the "blended librarian" who utilizes the librarian's skills, knowledge, and relationships in more of an educational role.[10] Although all of the embedded service areas previously mentioned can still be used, importance is also given to digital learning materials, a variety of multimedia authoring tools, and utilization of social media in connecting with users.[11] It is the emphasis on using the online environment as an integral part of the education of students that sets blended librarianship apart from a more generalist point of view. Along the same lines of educational partners, embedded librarians may also work with faculty to write course assignments and to incorporate other research training exercises into the online classroom syllabus.[12] David Shumaker and Laura Ann Tyler suggest that embedded librarians should keep their user group updated with current news items pertaining to the course and gather information from the embedded experience as a whole to document the group's knowledge level, needs, and learning.[13] These embedded services incorporate a wide variety of tasks, all of which take time. The library liaison can be involved online at different commitment levels as the work schedule allows. An average embedded librarian spends five to seven hours a week with duties associated with just one course, so be realistic in work goals.[14] No one liaison can do everything. Choose what is the most effective of the many options available. Start with manageable embedded liaison assistance and expand the services slowly as time and efficiency allows.

One important area for embedded librarians continues to be information literacy instruction. Library instruction and research training conducted online can be challenging. However, this can be accomplished in a number of ways. Opening an online discussion forum is one option. This method has

Capella University Time-Saver Tip

At Capella University, embedded librarians cut and paste reoccurring answers to online post questions from a library "knowledge base." The answers are slightly modified to personalize the response but save time with creating online responses.

SOURCE: Erika Bennett and Jennie Simning, "Embedded Librarians and Reference Traffic: A Quantitative Analysis," *Journal of Library Administration* 50, no. 5 (2010): 454–55.

been utilized by the Community College of Vermont through an approach that involved a question-and-answer method in addition to posts on research strategies.[15] At Capella University (an all online institution) embedded librarians have their own "Ask A Librarian" discussion board.[16] Another method can involve the use of software programs for video conferencing (such as Wimba Classroom, eLecta Live, or Elluminate Live!) or webinars (such as Adobe Connect or InstantPresenter). This method of online information literacy instruction has been tried by Kent State University Geauga and Virginia Commonwealth University.[17] With this special video conferencing software, in addition to a visual connection to the librarian, PowerPoint, documents, and online navigation can be used to enhance the IL instruction. Online discussions, videoconferences, online tutorials, and webinars are all options available to embedded librarians. Regardless of format, liaisons should find a way to deliver IL instruction to online users. This may be the only opportunity for these students to learn these critical research skills.

Another method used to enhance the librarian's presence in courseware is by embedding links and helpful suggestions into the online classroom. This embedded information suggests to the students some relevant databases, research guides, citation guides, research tips, or books or media that may be helpful to their studies. For example, an embedded business librarian may add links to the databases Business Source Complete, LexisNexis Academic, or Business & Company Resource Center. The business liaison may provide research tips on finding information through books, e-books, and electronic resources on market analysis, consumer behavior, advertising, or business law, to mention a few areas. Adding links to the online course gives students one-click access to important library resources. Embedded tips

and suggestions may provide essential information to the student any time
of the day. Links also provide a set of research tools and information sources
that all students can easily access for assignment completion.

General reference and research assistance can be offered online as well.
This is typically done through an online communication method such as
chat, e-mail, and discussion boards. While a discussion board can be used
for IL instruction, this board is also an avenue for general questions students
may have for the librarian. It is here that answers can be provided for students about resources, citations, and validity of websites, just to name a few.
For those questions which may be perceived as embarrassing for the student,
private chat or e-mail communications should be available. The embedded
liaison should check the online course daily for student communications to
respond in a timely manner to students' questions.

Finally, embedded librarians can utilize quizzes and feedback questionnaires to measure the impact their services have on student learning. These
can be delivered during or after tutorials, after an online IL instructional session, and at the end of the course. For example, Blackboard Learn enables
tests, quizzes, polls, and surveys to be taken by students.[18] Through this feedback the library liaison can determine which activities are having a positive effect on learning and which may need to be changed. (Evaluations are
covered in depth in chapter 11.) It is good for the embedded liaison to keep
some course notes about positive and negative activities. Where did students
struggle? What could have been changed to make the online library support
better? What was the level of student understanding with library research?
These notes from both the liaison experiences and student feedback will be
useful for improvements the next time the course is taught.

Of all the librarians, it is only the embedded librarian who will have contact with many online learners. This connection is vital as distance education
grows in popularity. Because of this, an effort must be made to interact with
the students, even online. Support must be given in the areas of reference and
research tools, but daily contact through discussion boards and other online
learning avenues is a must. Use of online links, e-mail and chat communication, discussion boards, tip sheets, IL instruction, tutorials, and quizzes are
all methods the embedded liaison uses to assist and stay connected. While it
is still a virtual experience, the student who connects with the librarian will
improve research skills.[19] The fact that the librarian is not in a face-to-face
environment with the student does not mean learning cannot occur. Students

are more likely to reach out for continued librarian assistance, equally in both virtual and in-person environments, if the librarian interacts with them.[20] The library liaison should keep in mind that while embedding information is helpful, it is the relationship that still counts when assisting and supporting the classroom experience.

Online Embedment Checklist

☐ Information literacy instruction
☐ Links and tips
☐ Reference and research assistance
☐ Quizzes and feedback questionnaires

Classroom Embedment

A library liaison embedded into a classroom provides the opportunity to establish a more personal and direct relationship with the students. Unlike the challenge of connecting in a virtual world, the liaison embedded in a physical classroom will have face-to-face contact with the students. The liaison will be able to listen to class discussions, field student questions, and get a sense of both the victories and struggles of the students as the course unfolds. This information is essential to making the embedded liaison an effective facilitator in the class. Additionally, the prospect of forming personal relationships with some, if not all, of the students makes classroom embedment a great chance to improve the liaison's effectiveness.

The opportunity to work directly with an instructor to help create an assignment brings its own challenges and rewards. Perhaps the greatest advantage that an embedded librarian brings to the role of assignment creation is an awareness of library resources that can help to alleviate student frustration. For example, at the University of Houston, several librarians coteach with faculty and are able to steer faculty to good library resources in addition to reviewing and grading library-related assignments.[21] If a member of the faculty creates an assignment and it is difficult to find research resources (which sometimes do not exist at all), this can be very difficult for students. Additionally, it can put the reference librarian in an awkward position. A close working relationship with an instructor, good communication when creating or reviewing an assignment, and checking if the assignment's research requirements can be met will alleviate this type of quandary for students.

Often the role of the embedded librarian is one where the expertise that is called upon is that of a research adviser when creating assignments for students or assisting faculty with projects. Assignment assistance may include how to guide students in narrowing topic ideas, beginning research, as well as finding and evaluating resources. For example, as part of a given assignment, students could be asked to submit five credible sources in correct bibliographic form. When working on research projects, Jake Carlson, a Purdue University research scientist, and Ruth Kneale, National Solar Observatory systems librarian, suggest that the embedded research librarian be a "team player" with both faculty and administration.[22] This type of liaison also must take risks and reach outside of his or her comfort zone because this is a fairly new area of library work involving new research, disciplines, and duties.[23] While sometimes difficult and challenging, the role of research adviser for both classroom assignments and research projects is often where an embedded librarian can really shine and initiate worthwhile liaison work.

In the most ideal cases, the embedded librarian is a part of planning course objectives and course content. In some cases, this inclusion of information literacy and research requirements may begin in curriculum meetings for new course development. They may also be discussed in faculty meetings that liaisons attend. However, most likely, the embedded librarian is dealing with an established course and syllabus where elements of the assignment may need refining. This requires a meeting with the instructor prior to the start of the course to discuss assignments and offer suggestions. If the relationship formed with the faculty member who is teaching the class is strong, this level of embedded assistance may be possible. Because faculty members may be unaware of this type of assistance, the librarian must gently set the tone. For those instructors who have incorporated information literacy into previous classes, the changes should go smoothly. This assistance with classroom assignment creation is yet another way the embedded librarian can create added value and impress upon the faculty and the students the librarian's worth.

In addition to traditional roles, there are many different forms of work an embedded librarian can take on. These tasks may be out of the normal realm of library work. For example, if the instructor asks for technical help, such as with designing a class web page or initiating and monitoring a class blog, in doing these tasks, the liaison may encounter a learning curve. There can be a great deal of variance in what each institution requires of librarians and whether there are other support staff who may be able to help with these types of requests. It is imperative to keep in mind that any help provided to the instructor and the students can fit into the role of an embedded librarian. However, some prudence should be taken to maximize the time and effort given. It can be a good idea to discuss with the faculty member previous to the class what the requirements are for the role of an embedded librarian. In turn, the liaison can communicate what can be offered to the class. For example, one option for the embedded liaison is to offer to create a library or research guide for the class (discussed in more detail in chapter 9) that can improve communication and display information resources to students. As an embedded liaison, a wide range of duties may be required in the job.

In the role of an embedded liaison, often librarians will encounter a broader objective—elevated assistance. Elevated assistance involves high-level analysis in the process of providing assistance. According to Shumaker and Talley, in a 2009 Special Libraries Association study, the top embedded liaison roles are training on information sources, ready reference or fact checking, topical research, resource development, news alerting or awareness, how-to manuals and pathfinders, and evaluating and synthesizing literature.[24] To provide this support, embedded liaisons are involved in "collaboration" with others and "analysis" of information and processes.[25] This requires the liaison to, not simply provide information literacy instruction or links, but to explore and uncover information, synthesize and filter research, analyze data, and then mold the information into a form useful to students and faculty. The role of an embedded librarian goes well beyond simply offering students a pipeline to information resources and is sometimes akin to the role played by librarians in special libraries such as law and medical libraries. [26]

Finally, actively working with a student beyond his or her awareness of information sources requires time and often an understanding of the individual's deep information needs. Assisting with these personal informational needs will help the students throughout their lives. Working closely with a students, embedded librarians have the opportunity to encourage consideration and understanding of how they might move forward in their chosen field. These librarians also will show them how information and their relationship to information will play a major role in their lives. For example, making students aware of the importance of gaining access to the news or top performers in their field through Twitter can enlighten them about this concept. An awareness of industry trends and the ability to summarize research in their chosen profession increase employability and set the tone for the future importance of this information skill set. As pointed out by R. David Lankes in his book *The Atlas of New Librarianship*, "The mission of librarians is to improve society through facilitating knowledge creation in their communities."[27] If one takes this mission to heart, then merely pointing to resources does not suffice. Embedded library liaison roles offered here help to explain this aspect of librarianship and shed light on the importance of lifelong learning. While it can be of the utmost importance to help a student through the immediate needs of a current assignment, one should not lose sight of some of the larger roles that a librarian can play in a student's life.

For those librarians embedded in a classroom, the chance for personal contact and learning is huge. Preplanning and review of assignments with the professor will allow for improved learning as the course progresses. Liaison roles of helping with research tips, assignments, information literacy, and research throughout the class are typical. This work may involve elevated assistance with analysis, synthesis, and formatting of information. All of this work results in students' understanding of how information can help personally and professionally in their lives. The role of a classroom-embedded liaison is intimate, dynamic, and varied. Be prepared to make a difference!

Classroom Embedment Checklist

- [ ] In-person relationship
- [ ] Assignment creation
- [ ] Research advisor
- [ ] Course planning
- [ ] Elevated assistance
- [ ] Deep information needs

Department Embedment

One step deeper into the embedment process comes when library liaisons take up residence within an academic department. While this type of embedded librarianship may not be seen by first-year liaisons, it is a growing concept in academic libraries. This type of embedded librarian service may involve select scheduled hours of the week in addition to work in the library itself or may mean a total relocation into the specific academic department the liaison represents. Either way, the time spent in this environment takes the library liaison one step closer to inclusion in the academic arena. It is here that these liaisons build a "collaborative relationship" with faculty members to an even greater degree than embedded classroom liaisons do.[28] Departmentally, embedded librarians become accepted as team members. Because their physical location is among the faculty on a daily basis, the number of opportunities for interaction and assistance increase. From simple, casual conversations to recognizing opportunities for research assistance, these liaisons are in the middle of the department's action.

The departmentally embedded librarian can get an insider's view of the department's needs that no other outsider can. Armed with this information and proximity, the liaison can support the department faculty in a number of ways. Assistance with research, interlibrary loans, journal selection, citations, and management styles were among the many areas business librarian Linda Bartnik found herself involved with at Murray State University.[29] Since 1994, Virginia Tech's College Library Program has integrated library liaisons directly into various departments on campus. This structure allows the embedded liaisons to better assist with collection development, research needs, assignment creation, information literacy instruction, literature reviews, grant projects, and class web page creation.[30] The Johns Hopkins University Welch Medical Library has been a leader in embedded librarianship. They have eleven embedded librarians serving the university as they move toward an all-electronic collection.[31] Working within the departments allows the Welch embedded librarians (or "informationists" as they are termed) to not only deliver information at the point of need but also collaborate with staff and instructors.[32] These are examples of departmentally embedded librarians in action. While these duties are not necessarily different from those performed by a library liaison located at the library, the frequency and depth of the inquiries increase, especially if the liaison is located in high-traffic areas of the department.[33]

Because there is no substitute for in-person interaction with faculty, a liaison embedded in a department has a unique experience. The opportunities for both verbal and nonverbal communication make this kind of embedment a ripe opportunity for library assistance. Departmentally embedded librarians need to fully understand their reporting structure and often have

Welch Medical Library Informationist Services

The informationists (embedded librarians) at Welch assist clinicians, clinician educators, researchers, lab groups, administrators, staff, and students. Some of the areas of assistance include the following:

- Research and patient care questions
- Practice standards creation with research
- Clinical research funding sources
- Department-specific resource presentations
- Best journals for publication
- Patent searches
- Citation and bibliography guidance

SOURCE: Welch Medical Library, "Informationist Services for Selected User Groups," http://welch.jhmi.edu/welchone/Informationist-Services-for-Selected-User-Groups.

to balance the demands of both the library and the academic department.[34] Embedded librarians can also lose touch with peers and the library community when their time is spent in academic departments.[35] An effort must be made to stay connected with the library and other librarians. However, if spending time embedded in a department becomes available, embrace the opportunity. Get to know the faculty like never before. Use this connection to assist, strengthen, and nurture the library's relationship with these individual departments.

Department Embedment Checklist

- ☐ Collaborative relationships
- ☐ Insider's perspective
- ☐ Specialized assistance
- ☐ In-person interaction

Conclusion

From orientation meetings to communication with faculty, interaction and connections play an important role in the liaison duties. The opportunity to work even more closely with faculty and students as an embedded librarian (especially in the physical classroom setting) allows for another level of collaboration. While there may be some consternation about moving out of the "comfort zone" of the library, the role of the embedded librarian can be seen as outreach and growth as the concept of "the library as place" continues to morph and in many cases expands in value. Embedded librarians of today can connect with students directly through an online and in-person classroom presence like never before. It is here at the point of learning in the educational process that embedded librarians assist with library-related assignments and needs. This outreach into student learning is proactive and involved. With embedded librarians in departments connecting with faculty members as never before, this coexistence expands the use of library services and personalizes the liaison work. Embedded librarians are becoming coworkers instead of "addendum librarians" in another building on campus. The opportunity to add value to the classroom and facilitate use of library resources is magnified by the work of embedded library liaisons.

NOTES

1. Erika Bennett and Jennie Simning, "Embedded Librarians and Reference Traffic: A Quantitative Analysis," *Journal of Library Administration* 50, no. 5 (2010): 444.

2. David Shumaker, "Who Let the Librarians Out?," *Reference & User Services Quarterly* 48, no. 3 (2009): 240.

3. David Shumaker and Mary Talley, "Models of Embedded Librarianship" (paper presented at the Special Libraries Association, June 16, 2009), www.sla.org/PDFs/SLA2009/ModelsofEmbeddedLibrarianshipJune162009.pdf: 40.

4. Barbara Dewey, "The Embedded Librarian: Strategic Campus Collaborations," *Resource Sharing & Information Networks*, 17, no. 1–2 (2004): 6.

5. Phyliss Rudin, "No Fixed Address: The Evolution of Outreach Library Services on University Campuses," *Reference Librarian* 49, no. 1 (2008): 61; David Shumaker and Laura Ann Tyler, "Embedded Library Services: An Initial Inquiry into Practices for Their Development, Management, and Delivery" (paper presented at the Special Libraries Association Annual Conference, Denver, Colorado, June 6, 2007), www.sla.org/pdfs/sla2007/ShumakerEmbeddedLibSvcs.pdf: 12.

6. Rudin, "No Fixed Address," 62–67.

7. Rebecca Hedreen, "Embedded Librarians," *Frequently Questioned Answers* (blog), http://frequanq.blogspot.com/2005/04/embedded-librarians.html.

8. Ibid.

9. John Shank and Nancy Dewald, "Establishing Our Presence in Courseware: Adding Library Services to the Virtual Classroom," *Information Technology and Libraries* 22, no. 1 (2003), www.ala.org/lita/ital/22/1/shank.

10. John D. Shank and Steven Bell, "Blended Librarianship: [Re]Envisioning the Role of Librarian as Educator in the Digital Information Age," *Reference & User Services Quarterly* 51, no. 2 (2011): 106.

11. Ibid., 108.

12. Shumaker and Tyler, "Embedded Library Services," 5.

13. Ibid., 2–3.

14. Bennett and Simning, "Embedded Librarians," 454.

15. Victoria Matthew and Anne Schroeder, "The Embedded Librarian Program," *EDUCAUSE Review Online*, June 2012, www.educause.edu/ero/article/embedded -librarian-program.

16. Robin Veal and Erika Bennett, "The Virtual Library Liaison: A Case Study at an Online University," *Journal of Library Administration* 49, no. 1–2 (2009): 163.

17. Mary Hricko, "Developing Library Instruction for Distance Learning, Middle Tennessee State University" (paper presented at the Mid-South Instructional Technology Conference, April 9, 2001), http://frank.mtsu.edu/~itconf/proceed01/24. html; Peter Kirlew, "Enhancing Synchronous Online Library Instruction Services in Blackboard Using the Wimba Live Classroom System," *Special Libraries Association*, 2007, www.sla.org/pdfs/sla2007/kirlewonlinelibinstrsvcs.pdf.

18. Blackboard, Inc., "Products-Feature Showcase," *Blackboard Learn*, www.blackboard .com/Platforms/Learn/Products/Blackboard-Learn/Teaching-and-Learning/Feature -Showcase.aspx#inspired-vista.

19. David Shumaker, "What's the ROI of Embedded Librarianship—Part 1," *The Embedded Librarian* (blog), http://embeddedlibrarian.com/2011/01/.

20. Bennett and Simning, "Embedded Librarians," 450.

21. Alexandra Simmons, "Librarians and Faculty Working Together at the University of Houston," *Texas Library Journal* 85, no. 4 (2009): 127.

22. Jake Carlson and Ruth Kneale, "Embedded Librarianship in the Research Context," *College and Research News* 72, no. 3 (2011): 168.

23. Ibid., 168–69.

24. Shumaker and Talley, "Models of Embedded Librarianship," 26.

25. David Shumaker and Mary Talley, "Models of Embedded Librarianship Final Report," *Special Libraries Association*, June 30, 2009, www.sla.org/pdfs/Embedded LibrarianshipFinalRptRev.pdf: 34.

26. Shumaker and Talley, "Models of Embedded Librarianship," 26.

27. R. David Lankes, *The Atlas of New Librarianship* (Massachusetts: MIT Press, 2011), 15.

28. Shumaker, "Who Let the Librarians Out?," 241.

29. Martin A. Kesselman and Sarah B. Watstein, "Creating Opportunities: Embedded Librarians," *Journal of Library Administration* 49, no. 4 (2009): 390.

30. University Libraries, "College Librarian Program and Contacts," *Virginia Polytechnic Institute and State University*, www.lib.vt.edu/instruct/clprg.html.

31. Welch Medical Library, "Informationist Program," *William H. Welch Medical Library*, http://welch.jhmi.edu/welchone/node/19.

32. Blair Anton, "The Welch Medical Library of 2012—Wherever You Are," *Library Connect*, http://libraryconnect.elsevier.com/articles/roles-professional-develop ment/2011-03/welch-medical-library-2012-%E2%80%94-wherever-you-are.

33. A. Ben Wagner, "On-Site Reference Services and Outreach: Setting Up Shop Where Our Patrons Live" (presented at the Special Libraries Association National Annual Meeting, June 8, 2004), www.acsu.buffalo.edu/~abwagner/Outreach-SLAPaper-2004 .htm.

34. Annette Haines, "Out in Left Field: The Benefits of Field Librarianship for Studio Arts Program" (paper presented at the ARLIS/NA Annual Conference, March 2003), http:// web.simmons.edu/~mahard/Haines%202004.pdf.

35. Rudin, "No Fixed Address," 70.

Library Guides

Pathfinders, bibliographic pointers, research guides, subject guides, course guides, and LibGuides are just a few of the names for the research assistance tools librarians have been creating that have been communicated in written form and now are offered online. The goal of each is connecting users to resources, which belies their value to the library liaison. The origin of such guides as "finding lists" and "reading lists" began in the early twentieth century as library collections expanded.[1] Because of the larger number of offerings to patrons, librarians began to make suggestion lists for them to find information and interesting readings.[2] The actual use of the word *pathfinder* did not take place until 1972 when Marie Canfield of the Massachusetts Institute of Technology provided a set format for compiling these information lists.[3] In 1996 the use of pathfinders went electronic and online research guides began.[4] Many academic library websites were designed with the primary goal of showcasing the research resources that students were advised by assignments to use. A variety of methods for creating online guides was implemented across the country, including OCLC's Cooperative Online Resource Catalog, which had 1,700 pathfinders by 2001.[5] (This later evolved into the modern OCLC Connexion.) The lack of standardization and simplicity in the online environment eventually led to LibGuides. Created by

Springshare in 2007, LibGuides are tailored to be flexible and personalized when presenting resources. LibGuides currently serve 3,400 libraries in 35 countries.[6] Both open source options and LibGuides will be covered in this chapter along with some practical tips for creating research guides.

Library Guides—Best Practices for Design and Purpose

Library guides have gained in popularity and have also spawned numerous efforts for best practices in approaches to their creation, usability, and optimization. It is beyond the scope of this book to attempt to detail all of the ways to improve the design and presentation of online information. Despite this, it is a good idea to be acquainted with tips for practical and basic creation of online information. It is good practice to spend some time before creating research guides to become familiar with these concepts which make the guides attractive, organized, and usable.

Depending on the size of the staff and the various job responsibilities, designating a lead person as a guide administrator can be beneficial. Guide administrators should control who has access to web pages and play a role in the guidelines for research guide creation. They should oversee the general administration of guides in this supervisory capacity. Additionally, some libraries form administrative committees prior to guide implementation to assist during rollout and marketing. It cannot be reiterated enough that a quality commitment to planning and keeping up with standardizing the look of the guides throughout pays dividends when promoting them and offers students a more consistent and less daunting user experience.

Because there are often numerous creators of content within a library, a "best practice" for uniformity is necessary. This web page consistency also helps with usability. Uniform guide creation starts with a guide design plan and procedures for creating a guide page. The creation of a plan avoids redundancies when creating content. This can be done in the form of a checklist other users must follow when creating, publishing, and publicizing guides. Items such as the colors of the guide pages and background, number of columns on a guide page, and the type of content (text based versus media) can be part of this planning. Alisa C. Gonzalez and Theresa Westbrook from New Mexico University took some time once they acquired LibGuides to address "purpose, organization, and plan; faculty involvement; audience awareness; and evaluation and assessment."[7] They noted that guide usage would require constant "attention and maintenance" through "regular assessment."[8] This particular point cannot be stressed enough. Students are usually driven to using library guides for a particular assignment need and generally do not have a deep understanding of the guides as a persistent resource. This is one of the reasons why the information needs to be constantly reviewed and updated. Some guide owners establish a policy whereby the guides must be updated on a monthly or bimonthly basis for a fresh user experience. Often this assessment of guide use leads to new ways of designing them. For example, some guide creators have changed from using more text-based landing pages for the first page of a guide to more image-based ones for ease of use. For those using LibGuides, once these policies, procedures, and standards are in place, share them with LibGuide creators to help with uniform design that improves usability. Springshare (LibGuide's parent company) also helps with this by letting templates be created that can standardize the look of new guides. The leading best practice is to take some time after the guide software is acquired to plan, document, and share a strategy that will lead to greater uniformity, usability, and wise use of resources before creating any published or "live" guides.

Analyzing what makes an online resource accessible, easy to find and use, and positioned at the forefront of a student's mind when accessing information is not an easy task. Brenda Reeb and Susan Gibbons point out that the most effective and well-used guides are those which take into consideration the specific needs of students.[9] They document a number of surveys and studies showing that many are created and yet students either find the access or the search engine design too complex and thus, abandon guide use.[10] In summation, they note the following:

> To affect student learning, a librarian must meet the student on the student's experiential terms. Once a connection is established, the librarian can then bring the student to a place of broader knowledge, awareness of content, and greater information literacy.[11]

Although it can seem to be quite self-evident, the idea of directed resources is commonly overlooked. Many librarians are susceptible to creating innumerable subject-specific guides that initially appear worthwhile from the librarian point of view of valuable resources on a specific subject. These librarians wrestle with how broad or narrow the subject information should be, and whether the librarian is helping or hand-holding the student in content creation. However, when some thought is given to how and why students may use the resource, especially when finding it on their own, a librarian may soon realize that specific assignment and course guides are best. These types of guides provide a more directed need.

Design strategy is a critical component to guide success. Librarians at the University of British Columbia created a Subject Guides Working Group that performed a survey which in turn developed a "Top Ten" list of student recommendations for their guides:

1. Clean and simple layout
2. Annotations
3. Search features
4. Embedded instruction
5. Easily understood content
6. Librarian contact info
7. Tabs
8. Citation info
9. Section headings
10. Page length to minimize scrolling[12]

One example of a LibGuide page that provides some of these elements is the Self-Help Books Guide for Johnson & Wales University, which strives for easily understood content with clean and simple layout and the use of tabs and section headings (see figure 9.1; http://jwucharlotte.libGuides.com/selfhelp).

Good points to remember from website page design, as suggested by Jakob Nielsen and Hoa Loranger, include incorporating one click to return to the home page, limiting wordy paragraphs, use of bold or underlining to indicate links, and consistency in overall page design.[13] For the design of LibGuides, its parent company Springshare also offers a number of good resources on its website that can help improve the creative strategy. The first of these is a LibGuide that Springshare has created which links to other institutions' LibGuides that they find to be well designed and engaging. Their "best of" guide is a good resource to use to help get a feel for good standards (figure 9.2). Some of these guides have also been nominated by the LibGuides community for inclusion. As a supplement to this resource, Springshare adds

FIGURE 9.1

Johnson & Wales University Self-Help subject page

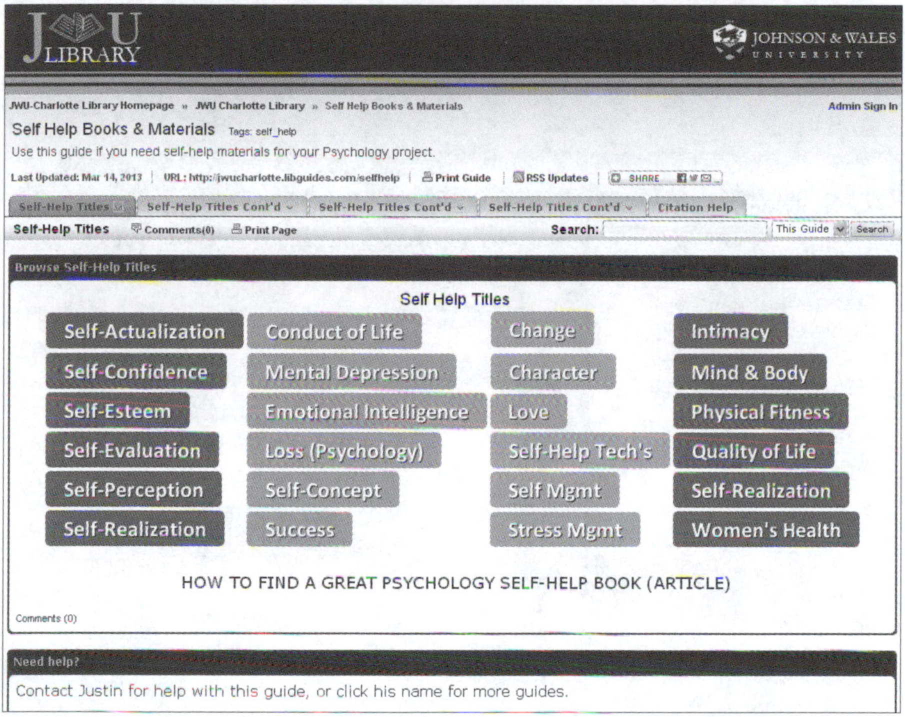

Reprinted with permission.

another guide that defines and points to resources that help to develop best practices and style guidelines (figure 9.3). The combination of these two company tools can be a great help with planning, creating, and presenting LibGuides.

Finally, an awareness of communication with students through research guide pages by the library liaison is necessary. Adding a chat widget to the librarian profile or to each guide front page is a way to reach students. This chat widget can enhance real-time communications with the library liaison. Additionally, when creating guides directed toward students, it is good practice to refrain from using library jargon as much as possible. Words that librarians are familiar with, such as *Boolean* or *bibliographic*, may cause consternation in students and potentially thwart use. Names for links should be easy to understand and communicate what information can be found when

FIGURE 9.2
Springshare Community "Best Of" LibGuide

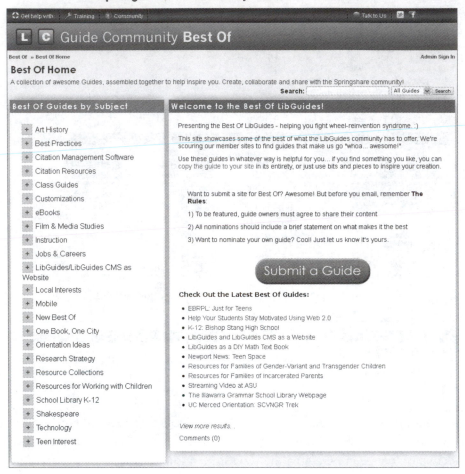

Reprinted with permission.

clicked so users scanning the page can pick up quickly the information they need.[14]

For online research guides to be successful, they should be led by an administrator. Just like general web pages, guides' pages must be simple to navigate but also contain relevant information for the user. Student and faculty needs must be taken into consideration. Library liaisons creating guides should be aware of the best design practices and explore sample guides as well. Remember, research guides are useless unless utilized.

FIGURE 9.3
Springshare "Best Practices" LibGuide

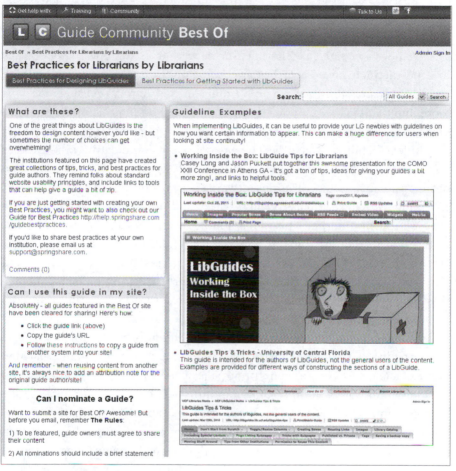

Reprinted with permission.

LibGuides

Technology that survived the boom of the 1990s was given the name "Web 2.0" in 2004 by Tim O'Reilly and Dale Dougherty.[15] Surviving software was "collaborative . . . interactive, [and] dynamic."[16] Two years later in 2006, the name "Library 2.0" was used by Michael Casey in his *LibraryCrunch* blog for library technology with these same characteristics.[17] On the wave of this collaborative software trend for libraries, Springshare developed and released

LibGuides in 2007. The Web 2.0 that focused on user-created and user-centric content had paved the way for a library product which "combines the best features of blogs, wikis, and social networks into one package designed specifically for libraries."[18] LibGuides were born.

LibGuides are touted as differing from earlier incarnations of subject guides in a few distinct ways. First, they are hosted on Springshare's servers, which takes this responsibility away from librarians and library websites. Perhaps more important is that libraries are not dependent on their institution's information technology department for help when creating these types of resources for students, staff, and faculty. The ease of use when creating LibGuides is also a factor in their popularity. As of this writing, almost 250,000 pages had been created using the LibGuide software.[19] From a purposeful point of view, LibGuides provide a "doorway" to research and information.[20] They can also be used to link Internet sites, government resources, databases, and other useful information for students and faculty.[21] LibGuide updates to the code are automatically "pushed out" by Springshare. This means new features and changes to the software are also part of the yearly subscription fee. A perceptive library liaison would see the value of LibGuides as a platform for connecting and assisting users with information resources.

LibGuides use a very basic design when a guide is created, which is also an attractive selling point for librarians who are averse to large learning curves. The creator has a blank front page when initiating a guide and can divide it into a maximum of three columns. Within the columns, a guide creator populates a box or boxes with various types of information. These boxes range from text boxes to media boxes for embedding videos to a content box for library books from your catalog or ready-made Google content boxes. Librarian profile boxes with contact information are also an option to personalize pages and facilitate communication. Boxes within a LibGuide page are simply titled and filled with any relevant content as chosen by the librarian. Because boxes within a LibGuide page are easily manipulated, updating guides with current content from the library resources or outside news links is possible.[22] Finally, LibGuides offer not only the ability to copy content from the set created at the primary institution but also the capability of copying any of the information (with permission) contained within any institution's LibGuides.

Feedback is another feature of LibGuides that is useful. Creators have the ability to insert a survey poll into one of the page boxes. A link for comments on the LibGuide page itself can also be utilized.[23] Usage stats for not only the pages created but also the links on the pages can be monitored.[24] This is critical feedback so the liaison librarian can know whether the guide is being utilized and what information is being accessed by the students.

An important decision that needs to be made when beginning the creation of a guide is what type of focus it will have when students access it. Is the guide's primary content related to a certain subject, such as history or accounting? Or is the guide focused on a singular course and will offer students help with their research resources for it? Perhaps the main thrust of the guide is that it can help with a specific assignment and can be presented during a library instruction class as a way to centralize resources. This type of decision about the purpose of the guide is covered in more detail later in this chapter. Because research guides have the potential to be first points of contact for students and faculty members, it is important for the liaison to take some time to consider them. In chapter 2, the importance of becoming a subject expert was discussed. The opportunity to present this expertise is a hallmark of research guide creation. The prospect of directing students (and any other audience) to valuable information as well as learning how to use the resources that your library owns are very beneficial to the liaison role. The focus of the LibGuide page must be determined before its creation.

Evolving out of the Web 2.0 and Library 2.0 revolution, LibGuides have become a popular option for academic libraries when relaying information and creating resources guides. The simplicity of the software makes updates and adding a variety of Web 2.0 options easy for any librarian. Choosing a focus for each page and planning in advance are always recommended. Finally, checking on web page usage and feedback allows the library liaison to make adjustments to the material to maximize the LibGuide usage.

LibGuide Checklist

- ☐ Guide administrator
- ☐ Concepts for usability
- ☐ Student needs
- ☐ Design strategy
- ☐ Advantages of LibGuides
- ☐ Basic design
- ☐ Feedback opportunities
- ☐ Focus of pages

Marketing Research Guides

The marketing of research guides can be a primary factor in their success or failure. Innovative ideas can help to publicize library resources and drive students to the research guides. From the liaison point of view, remember that guides publicizing the electronic resources and the library services available are only two of the advantages. Guides also promote the library liaisons and their expertise. Research guides are a method for liaison librarians to communicate to the students and faculty their subject specialties and to relay their vast subject knowledge. Reference guides are also used in library instruction as a way to show students a collection of resources that may help them with assignments and projects. Because the guides are available anywhere and anytime, their availability at the point of need is reinforced in the library instruction class. Additionally, the librarian profile placed within affords the opportunity to display contact items, office hours, calendars, and social media connectors.

Library guides can promote the overall library program. The Voskuyl Library at Westmont College in Santa Barbara, California, uses LibGuides to define and promote its library liaison program (figure 9.4). In this instance the liaison program is explained and library liaisons with contact information are highlighted. This illustrates that guide pages can be used for all kinds of information and marketing of services. Guides are not necessarily restricted to simply resources pages.

In some measure, the very definition of a research guide makes it a marketing tool for library resources. However, once the guides have been created, it can be a quandary to determine ways to promote the guides so that audiences will use them. Many libraries use prominent images, banners, and links to drive students to the home page of the guides. The guide home page acts as an entry point to other guides and is often used by some libraries as the main web page for the library itself (rather than a subset information point). A link to research guides can also be placed within online learning management systems, such as Blackboard, Moodle, and Sakai, to direct students immediately to these resources. Duke University places library liaison contact information and resource links directly in online Blackboard courses for increased collaboration and interaction between students and librarians.[25] Links can also be placed in RSS feeds and other social media announcements if these are a communication method used by the library. Noteworthy in

FIGURE 9.4
Westmont College Voskuyl Library Liaison Program page

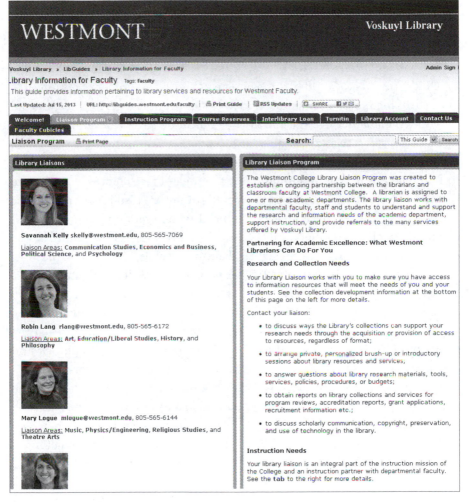

Reprinted with permission.

relation to the liaison role, the article "The Next Generation Research Guide: LibGuides Training and Marketing at SFSU" begins by taking into consideration the many ways in which to market LibGuides. In 2007 San Francisco State University switched sixty-six research guides from HTML to LibGuides and marketed them through home page links, Twitter, Facebook, blogs, and faculty e-mails.[26] They determined that e-mail resulted in the highest impact on use and was directly related to the established relationships between librarians and faculty members.[27] The study found a 67 percent increase in research guide usage compared to only a 27 percent increase in a set of controlled guides not marketed through the website and social media.[28]

For ease of use when searching and finding guides, LibGuides software implements a tactic that became popular with the tools and software associated with the interactivity of Web 2.0—page tagging. When publishing a LibGuide, the creator is offered the choice of adding a number of options to a guide, making it easier for students to find. One option is giving the guide an easy-to-remember term at the end of your LibGuide site's web address—what Springshare refers to as a "friendly URL." Another is associating a guide with a predefined (determined by the librarian) category that can make it easier to find when browsing for guides. Last, the idea of tags comes in. Similar to the concept of categories, due to the fact that they are also predefined terms, assigned tags are keywords that can be used when searching for guides. For example, when publishing a LibGuide on baking and pastry resources, the guide creator can assign tags, such as "baking," "cakes," "cookies," "pastry," "pies," and "plated-desserts," so that when a user searches with one of those terms, the guide will be in the result set. Page tagging allows the creator to define the terms that will useful for those searching for information.

Research guide creation is not enough. Liaison librarians must reach the user through strategic marketing ideas. Placement of links to guides and research resources in courseware, e-mails, and other social networking methods is one option available for marketing. Finding research guides through page tagging once within the library site is also a useful tool for the end user. Additionally, marketing implies the use of relationship building between library liaisons and the users. Utilizing liaison photographs and contact information will help build this bond and, in turn, the reliance of faculty and students on library resources.

Research Guide Marketing Checklist

- ☐ Library services and resource promotion
- ☐ Marketing through courseware
- ☐ Marketing through social networking
- ☐ Page tagging

Interesting and Inventive LibGuide Uses

LibGuide's versatility has been put to the test in many different ways. The library liaison should take note of the myriad ways in which LibGuides can be used to reach out to students and faculty. As a seemingly natural fit, many libraries divvy up their LibGuide creation responsibilities along liaison lines. Therefore, the history or art liaison would be in charge of creating and maintaining LibGuides for that subject area. Oftentimes faculty members are invited to add to the guide creation.[29] Many libraries have taken the ease of use and quick construction of LibGuides and have found some inventive ways to explore their capabilities. The involvement of many creative individuals has resulted in unique LibGuide uses.

There have been cases where the library forgoes the idea of a library home page altogether and points users to the LibGuides home page as its website or default portal. Springshare notes a number of libraries that have done this here: http://springshare.com/libguides/academic/website.html. It is worth mentioning that Springshare also offers a product upgrade to LibGuides called LibGuides CMS that are more robust in their ability to target groups and may be even more appealing to the library liaison.

Another use of LibGuides is to link them to library instruction. One example is political science faculty at North Georgia College & State University using LibGuides to help students pinpoint pertinent information that addresses an information literacy standard created by the Association of College and Research Libraries.[30] Another approach used by Bloomsburg University of Pennsylvania came about when they designed an information literacy-focused tutorial and sought the use of the LibGuides platform for access.[31] Still another example to consider is that of Bradley Brazzeal, the library liaison to the Department of Forestry at Mississippi State University. In his article "Research Guides as Library Instruction Tools," he finds that "incorporating features that correspond directly to elements of a library instruction session" can be another tactic to engage the audience.[32] Brazzeal concludes that "research guides are not a substitute for the personal instruction received at the reference desk or in library instruction sessions, but they are one avenue of teaching users how to use library resources and services effectively."[33] Last, Jeanne Galvin sums up the use of research guides as a supplement to instruction and echoes the concerns of Reeb and Gibbons when she asserts that "both print and electronic guides and pathfinders extend the library's educational role when they are placed in a context and given an appropriate label so that students see them as tools for specific needs."[34] Overall, LibGuides have been used with great success to supplement library instruction in the academic setting.

LibGuides can also be used to showcase faculty works. Grand Valley State University faculty librarians used LibGuides as a platform to showcase portfolios for their tenure and promotion process.[35] The liaisons ended up surmising that some librarians "who are more comfortable with a narrative format will likely choose Adobe Acrobat, while those librarians more conversant with principles of information architecture may gravitate toward using LibGuides."[36] Springshare has taken note of the many ways in which librarians have used their product and often develops these ideas into products, in this case, Scholar Guides.

An interesting use of LibGuides comes from the University of South Florida Library's Special & Digital Collections Department. These librarians showcased their special collections and digital initiatives through LibGuides. Although there were some hurdles and compromises, they maintained that "LibGuides is as versatile as Springshare's promotional materials assert that it is and that libraries can make much more robust use of this economical platform than they currently do."[37] Another example comes from the James P. Adams Library at Rhode Island College where a LibGuide is used to highlight the reading room, collection archives, and college archives.[38]

LibGuides can also be used in relation to conferences. Library liaisons can use a guide to list conferences. For example, the University of Oxford's psychology liaison lists the area conferences with website links for faculty members.[39] LibGuides can also be created to assist faculty members in conference poster creation as well as to inform them about poster archiving options at their institution when completed. It is interesting to see how the versatility of LibGuides can offer ways to reach out to different audiences in innovative ways.

One other way to think about LibGuides is to consider their use as a learning platform. The aforementioned case of Bloomsburg University of Pennsylvania adapting James Madison University's information literacy teaching resource called "Go for the Gold" to a guide is a good example of rethinking how to use LibGuides.[40] "Go for the Gold" was "self-instructed modules" to improve information literacy skills.[41] Although this does not appear to be extraordinarily noteworthy, it gave the library a chance to promote the tool to faculty and also move information that the library already had into a more suitable format to "quickly brand existing content."[42] LibGuides in technical colleges can help students prepare for tests for certifications as, for example, a paramedic, firefighter, or cosmetologist. The Northeastern Technical College uses LibGuides to link to its Learning Express Library to accomplish this.[43] LibGuides' use as a learning platform through tutorials and test links allows liaisons to target specific student populations with necessary assistance.

LibGuides and Springshare's other offerings have had a large impact on how liaison librarians present themselves, resources, and services. The ability to have ownership in the online world to connect to students and faculty makes this a tool that deserves the liaison's attention and commitment. The creative uses of LibGuides continue to expand. A large part of the appeal of this product is that it was developed by librarians and the company behind it is committed to developing and maintaining the connection to those roots. At a minimum, LibGuides provide yet another way for liaisons to relate to user needs in creative and unique ways.

Interesting and Inventive Uses Checklist

☐ Dividing liaison creation of pages
☐ No home page
☐ Coauthoring with faculty
☐ Supplement to library instruction
☐ Special collections showcase
☐ Use as a learning platform

Open Source Guides

Similar to the situation with tutorial software that was discussed in chapter 4, there are also some freely available research guide options. LibGuides itself can be generally referred to as content management software (CMS). From that perspective, other open source CMS-type software such as Drupal (http://drupal.org/home) and Wordpress (http://wordpress.com/) have been used by libraries as backbones for research guide creation, presentation, and curation. Both are basic website creators with the ability to do a variety of things, including content sharing, newsletters, podcasts, and blogs. One open source tool that is available as a download is called LibData, and it was created by the University of Minnesota Libraries. LibData offers three applications—Research QuickStart (pathfinders), CourseLib (course resource pages), and PageScribe (general web pages).[44] Another open source resource is SubjectsPlus (www.subjectsplus.com). This was created by Ithaca College to manage lists for subject or course guides, databases, suggestions, and library staff profiles.[45] Academic centers using SubjectsPlus include Concordia College, Georgia Southern University, and the University of Miami, among others.[46] Yet another open source option comes from Oregon State University Library. The OSU Library created Library à la Carte (http://alacarte.library .oregonstate.edu/home) as an open source system for library guides. The web pages of this software integrate chat, RSS feeds, catalogs, and databases.[47] While free, the downside for these open source systems is they require "considerable technical expertise" to install initially and maintain and are usually hosted on a local server.[48]

The main advantage of open software is that ongoing use is free. These options do offer software to users for website creation, pathfinders, course web pages, and other content-sharing options. For the most part, technological support must come from the institution using the freeware. However, Library à la Carte does offer updates and fixes through their blog, and SubjectsPlus offers a wiki for code changes. With all freeware, costs for implementation, maintenance, server space, and technical support must be factored in. As in all software decisions, taking some time to weigh all considerations is a valuable exercise, but open source options may be just the solution to guide creation.

Open Source Subject Guide Checklist

☐ Drupal and Wordpress website options
☐ LibData, SubjectsPlus, and Library à la Carte guide creators
☐ Freeware requires tech support and maintenance

Conclusion

Today, the use of electronic guides is standard for liaisons in academic libraries. While LibGuides have dominated the software in this area, freeware options are available as well. This software has been able to capitalize on the excitement of Web 2.0 technologies and librarians' initial joy with their low learning curve and creative freedom. As this original glow has worn off, librarians, particularly liaison librarians, began to assess their worth beyond mere subject post boards and have attempted to expand research guide uses. Springshare has developed the guide's capabilities and the integration with its other products as well as gaining a reputation for solid support. All of these factors have helped with LibGuides' popularity. Institutions should assign a research guide administrator or group in charge of creating a standardization guideline for use. User needs and usage should be at the forefront of all guide planning and implementation. At their core, as with many other library tools, electronic research guides are opportunities for liaisons to directly assist their patrons.

NOTES

1. Carla Dunsmore, "A Qualitative Study of Web-Mounted Pathfinders Created by Academic Business Libraries," *Libri* 52, no. 3 (2002): 138.

2. Ibid.

3. Lugina Vileno, "From Paper to Electronic, the Evolution of Pathfinders: A Review of the Literature," *Spectrum Library,* http://spectrum.library.concordia.ca/5591/1/LVileno_RSR_Vol35_No3.pdf: 4.

4. Ibid., 7.

5. Ibid.

6. "Home," *Springshare LLC,* www.springshare.com/.

7. Alisa C. Gonzalez and Theresa Westbrook, "Reaching Out with LibGuides: Establishing a Working Set of Best Practices," *Journal of Library Administration* 50, no. 5–6 (2010): 656.

8. Ibid., 654.

9. Brenda Reeb and Susan Gibbons, "Students, Librarians, and Subject Guides: Improving a Poor Rate of Return," *portal: Libraries and the Academy* 4, no. 1 (2004): 124.

10. Ibid., 125.

11. Ibid., 126.

12. Kimberley Hintz et al., "Letting Students Take the Lead: A User-Centred Approach to Evaluating Subject Guides," *Evidence Based Library and Information Practice* 5, no. 4 (2010): 45.

13. Jakob Nielsen and Hoa Loranger, *Prioritizing Web Usability* (Berkeley, CA: Nielsen Norman Group, 2006), 27, 30, 98.

14. Ibid., 192.

15. Tim O'Reilly, "Design Patterns and Business Models for the Next Generation of Software," *O'Reilly Media Inc.,* http://oreilly.com/web2/archive/what-is-web-20.html.

16. Jack Maness, "Library 2.0 Theory: Web 2.0 and Its Implications for Libraries," *Webology* 3, no. 2 (2006), article 25, www.webology.org/2006/v3n2/a25.html.

17. Ibid.

18. Ellie Bushhousen, "LibGuides," *Journal of the Medical Library Association* 97, no. 1 (2009), www.ncbi.nlm.nih.gov/pmc/articles/PMC2605035/: 68–69.

19. "Home," *Springshare LLC.*

20. Jonathan Miner and Ross Alexander, "LibGuides in Political Science: Improving Student Access, Research, and Information Literacy," *Journal of Information Literacy* 4, no. 1 (2010): 41.

21. Ibid.

22. Bushhousen, "LibGuides."

23. Ibid.

24. Ibid.

25. Emily Daly, "Embedding Library Resources into Learning Management Systems: A Way to Reach Duke Undergrads at Their Points of Need," *College & Research Libraries News* 71, no. 4 (2010): 209.

26. Nicole Allensworth, Hesper Wilson, and Diane T. Sands, "The Next Generation Research Guide: LibGuides Training and Marketing at SFSU," J. Paul Leonard Library, http://carl-acrl.org/Archives/ConferencesArchive/Conference10/2010proceedings/Nicole-Allensworth.pdf: 4–5.

27. Ibid., 5.

28. Ibid., 4.

29. Steven Shapiro, "Marketing the Library with Content Management Systems: A Case Study of Blackboard," *Library Hi Tech News* 29, no. 3 (2012): 10.

30. Miner and Alexander, "LibGuides in Political Science," 45.

31. Kathryn Yelinek et al., "Using LibGuides for an Information Literacy Tutorial," *College & Research Libraries News* 71, no. 7 (2010): 353.

32. Bradley Brazzeal, "Research Guides as Library Instruction Tools," *Reference Services Review* 34, no. 3 (2006): 358.

33. Ibid., 366.

34. Jeanne Galvin, "Alternative Strategies for Promoting Information Literacy," *Journal of Academic Librarianship* 31, no. 4 (2005): 352–57.

35. Laura Harris, Julie Garrison, and Emily Frigo, "At the Crossroads: Bringing the Tenure and Promotion Process into the Digital Age," *College & Research Libraries News* 70, no. 8 (2009): 465.

36. Ibid., 468.

37. Melanie Griffin and Barbara Lewis, "Transforming Special Collections through Innovative Uses for LibGuides," *Collection Building* 30, no. 1 (2011): 5.

38. Marlene Lopes, "Special Collections," *James P. Adams Library, Rhode Island College*, http://ric.libguides.com/specialcollections.

39. Karine Barker, "Oxford LibGuides Psychology: Conferences & Professional Societies," *University of Oxford Bodleian Libraries*, http://ox.libguides.com/content.php?pid =184341&sid=1638180.

40. JMU Academic Affairs, "2010–11 Graduate Catalog: Resources," *James Madison University*, www.jmu.edu/gradcatalog/10/general/resources.html.

41. Ibid.

42. Yelinek et al., "Using LibGuides for an Information Literacy Tutorial," 352.

43. "Database Tutorials," *Northeastern Technical College*, http://netc.libguides.com/ content.php?pid=210815&sid=1818043.

44. "LibData: Library Page Authoring Environment," *University of Minnesota Libraries*, http://libdata.sourceforge.net/.

45. "Home Page," *SubjectsPlus*, www.subjectsplus.com/index.php.

46. "Sites Using SubjectsPlus," *SubjectsPlus*, www.subjectsplus.com/wiki/index.php ?title=Sites_using_SubjectsPlus.

47. Library à la Carte, "Home Page," *Oregon State University Libraries*, http://alacarte .library.oregonstate.edu/home.

48. Federal Financial Institutions Examination Council, "Risk Management of Free and Open Source Software," *Federal Deposit Insurance Corporation*, www.fdic.gov/news/ news/financial/2004/FIL11404a.html.

Accreditation and New Courses

In addition to the more traditional duties, liaisons play a key role in other areas as well. Sometimes these "nonroutine" activities can be just as critical or even more important than tasks in which liaisons engage on a daily basis. Accreditation and new course development are two such areas in which liaisons may become involved. In their respective ways, both of these areas deal with learning standards and what is being taught to students. Accreditation represents the standards by which learning and subsequent degrees delivered by colleges and universities are judged to be worthy. A degree from an accredited institution means that it has met standards set forth by peers in the industry. It allows for students to transfer between institutions with a common knowledge base and also signals to students and their parents that the institution they are attending will give them a good education.[1] Accreditation of a program is also looked at by employers who seek to ensure that they hire graduates who have been exposed to an appropriate degree of rigor, such as that which is required by the accreditation process. Liaison librarians fortunate to play a role in new course development will be able to incorporate resources and learning standards to maximize student learning and also be aligned with both recommended accreditation and library association standards.

Accreditation and new course development do impact libraries and library liaisons. Since libraries are a key component to student learning and are one of the supporting structures of an institution's mission and vision, they become involved in accreditation. As liaisons, librarians teach students about information resources and also become partners in the learning process. The liaison librarians may also be involved in new course development, which impacts collection development and information literacy as well as other service-related areas such as interlibrary loan. Since the collection must support academic needs, its overall assessment is also wrapped into accreditation. Much of what liaison librarians do provides supporting evidence that the library is in step with the institution's academic goals.

Accreditation Overview

Accreditation began to play a widespread role in academic communities during the Korean War. It was in 1952 that the GI Bill (student loans for returning veterans) forced the U.S. secretary of education to recognize which institutions were providing attendees an adequate education.[2] The government allowed veteran student loans only at academic institutions accredited by the U.S. commissioner of education's office.[3] Accredited institutions became recognized as solid academic centers. From this beginning, the governing accreditation authority has evolved through several changes to reach the current overseeing organization—the Council for Higher Education Accreditation (CHEA).[4] CHEA oversees approximately 3,000 institutions with a 20-person board.[5] The organization describes itself as the "primary national voice for voluntary accreditation and quality assurance to the U.S. Congress and U.S. Department of Education."[6]

The U.S. Department of Education lists the accreditation agencies of postsecondary schools. There are six regional accreditation bodies in the United States:

- Middle States Association of Colleges and Schools (MSACS)
- Northwest Commission on Colleges and Universities (NWCCU)
- North Central Association of Colleges and Schools (NCACS)
- New England Association of Schools and Colleges (NEASC)

- SACS (Southern Association of Colleges and Schools) Commission on Colleges (COC)
- Western Association of Schools and Colleges (WASC)[7]

There are also several other accreditation bodies recognized by the Department of Education, which include the Accrediting Commission of Career Schools and Colleges; Distance Education and Training Council, Accrediting Commission; New York State Board of Regents, and the Commissioner of Education; and the Transnational Association of Christian Colleges and Schools.[8]

Besides the recognition of academic standards, accreditation also allows federal money to come to the institution. This is important to the college or university as a whole as well as to the library, whose budget is affected by these numbers. Today, the U.S. Department of Education determines whether or not an institution is entitled to federal assistance for its students. There are currently thirty-eight accrediting bodies that are recognized and entitle colleges and universities to participate in financial aid programs provided by the federal government.[9] The six regional academic accreditation bodies are included in this list. It is rare that any institution can survive today without loan programs, federal work-study grants, and other federal assistance.

The value and importance of accreditation for the vast majority of institutions of higher education in the United States is critical. In fact, without accrediting from relevant bodies, most institutions in the United States would have to make fundamental changes justifying their role in the higher education marketplace. Accreditation plays a key role in fostering high quality in higher education by making sure that colleges and universities adhere to reasonable standards agreed upon by experts in what has become the "industry" of higher education. This applies to everything from how records are kept, what library resources are available, and how teaching and programs are evaluated on an ongoing basis. As more and more for-profit educational entities have entered the field in recent decades, the greatest concern within higher education, the government, and the general public is the possibility that a school would water down its own internal standards in exchange for a quick return on investment.[10] Not-for-profit universities and colleges are also not immune to various pressures that could seek to reduce the quality of education which they provide. These schools are often caught between the need to make improvements and add programs while simultaneously containing the overall tuition costs for students. Last, public institutions face ever-increasing pressure as well as they seek to do more with less as state budgets are slashed or frozen. Again, this is often being done while states and communities rely ever more heavily upon the expansion of academic and technical training programs that seek to bolster the long-term health of a given city, state, or region. Accreditation is especially important to liaison librarians as they seek to maintain a high level of resources and assistance with regard to specific programs and courses while budgetary restrictions mount.

Beyond the federally recognized accreditation bodies are the many organizations that exist to accredit specific programs or degrees. Accreditation varies widely from that which pertains to specific programs to that which is more general, such as the regional accreditation bodies. For example, the International Council on Hotel, Restaurant, and Institutional Education's (CHRIE) Accreditation Commission for Programs in Hospitality Administration is one such body that provides an additional level of credence to the quality of a hospitality-related baccalaureate program of study at a given school. In addition to more specific information, the International CHRIE provides an excellent definition on its website of general accreditation. It states the following:

> Accreditation is a status granted to an educational institution or program
> that has been found to meet or exceed stated standards of educational
> quality. Accreditation is an activity that has long been accepted in the
> United States. . . . This system of accreditation has helped to ensure that
> post-secondary education in the United States maintains the highest qual-
> ity both in the field of education and in the field of research.[11]

The Accreditation Board for Engineering and Technology (ABET) recognizes institutions in the area of applied science and engineering.[12] The Association to Advance Collegiate Schools of Business (AACSB) accredits a variety of academic business programs and states that graduates of these associated programs are "more desirable to employers."[13] These are examples of secondary accreditation organizations that lend even more credibility to academic institutions.

While accreditation is a broader procedure pertaining to the overall quality of an institution of higher education, the library is an important piece of the process. Accreditation agencies incorporate library skills and services into their standards. For example, with regard to the aforementioned regional accrediting bodies, the New England Association of Schools and Colleges has eleven "Standards for Accreditation." The seventh standard is dedicated to library services. The general statement related to this component of accreditation follows:

> The institution provides sufficient and appropriate library and information resources. The institution provides adequate access to these resources and demonstrates their effectiveness in fulfilling its mission. The institution provides instructional and information technology sufficient to support its teaching and learning environment.[14]

Other associations and standards speak to the need for quality library services as well, such as those drafted by the Southern Association of Colleges and Schools Commission on Colleges as put forth in its "Principles of Accreditation: Foundations for Quality Enhancement." Its standards for the library can be found in section 3 of this document, which also highlights requirements for faculty, student affairs, and other key areas.[15] The Middle States Association of Colleges and Schools recognizes information literacy skills within the syllabi as well as "critical analysis and reasoning" and "technological competency."[16] The Northwest Commission on Colleges and Universities specifically mentions the use of library resources in their standards.[17] While not referring directly to library liaisons, regional accrediting standards strongly imply the need to develop and maintain strong partnerships between the library and faculty by building relationships with the goal of better connecting faculty and students to information resources and fostering information literacy skills.

Most academic librarians would consider accrediting standards to be fairly vague and thus rely more heavily on other organizational standards in preparation for an accreditation visit. Numerous sources exist for narrowing down toward a better understanding of what is necessary. One such resource regarding information literacy is the Association of College and Research Libraries' "Standards for Libraries in Higher Education." These standards provide specific guidelines illustrating the learning outcomes students are expected to achieve as they relate to the library and information literacy. These standards provide expected outcomes that demonstrate how the library supports the educational environment. These nine areas of impact include institutional effectiveness, intellectual freedom and user rights, educational role, information discovery, access to collections, management and resource allocation, skilled library personnel, and community and campus relations.[18] It should be noted that organizations such as the ACRL provide webinars and other types of training sessions for library liaisons related to these efforts. For example, in June 2012, the ACRL offered the webinar "Preparing for Accreditation: An Introduction for Librarians."[19] Liaisons could gain much greater understanding of library services and be more effective in their roles by participating in these types of activities and programs. The specialized ABET accreditation for engineering mentions that library services "must be adequate to support the scholarly and professional activities of the students and faculty."[20] The Accreditation Commission for Programs in Hospitality Administration (ACPHA), which works in conjunction with International CHRIE, has accreditation standards that include that the academic facility provide adequate library resources to support faculty and program needs.[21] Liaisons play their most critical role in ensuring that these recommended library standards are being achieved for the program areas for which they have been assigned responsibility. (It should be noted that a more general IL program that encompasses their areas may exist.) Therefore, regional accreditation provides a broad push toward high quality, but it is often standards established by the ALA, the ACRL, and subject-relevant organizations in conjunction with specific program area needs and requirements that provide more specific guidance.

Accreditation of an academic institution signifies that a standard of learning is being met. It is critical for the reputation of the institution as well as for federal funding. For liaison librarians, support of the learning environment relates directly to accreditation standards, many of which include required library services and resources. Library standards may come from accrediting bodies or through specific organizations such as the ACRL. These recommendations guide liaison librarians who support specific subject areas such as collection development, information literacy, and research skills. The liaison librarian's insight into and evidence of these supporting elements are necessary to meet accreditation standards. The need to prove the library's worth in the role of education puts liaison librarians at the forefront of accreditation assistance at the time of these reviews.

Importance/Overview of Accreditation Checklist

☐ Accrediting bodies
☐ Federal assistance
☐ Quality education standard
☐ Accreditation-specific organizations
☐ Library skills in accrediting standards
☐ Resources for library accreditation standards

Accreditation Meetings/Visits

Accrediting teams usually consist of a panel of experts. Often they are administrators from peer institutions with significant experience in higher education who volunteer their time and energy to assist the regional accrediting body in its processes. These individuals come from a wide variety of backgrounds and usually include one person who either works in or is very familiar with libraries at his or her institution. Associations such as the NEASC, through the work done by these teams to evaluate peer institutions, commonly certify schools for ten years at a time, with an interim visit at the five-year mark. Another example is the ACPHA, which accredits every seven years, with accreditation teams consisting of executives from lodging, restaurant, and public industries.[22] An accreditation review always takes place on a timeline set by industry peers.

A typical accreditation visit will usually require that any and all paperwork and activities of the library, including library liaison activities, be documented. In preparation for this meeting, the library liaisons should have a summary of liaison work completed and under way and both print and electronic copies of all documentation associated with liaison work. In its most minimal circumstances, this would include a summary of the liaison efforts in the areas of collection development, technology assistance, information literacy instruction, and embedded assistance. For example, a library liaison in a collection development role might need to assess a collection by simply counting books or other resources related to a specific subject area. This can be done fairly easily using a modern ILS. (One could count the number of titles available within a specific call number range.) Inasmuch as this was how program areas were assessed many years ago, however, changes in technology and the need for qualitative and expert assessment of resources make simply counting resources less useful than it was in the past. If any additional paperwork exists giving specifics of efforts by liaisons, this too would be provided. These statistics could be anything from how often departmental meetings were attended outside the library to the number of IL sessions conducted that were tailored toward the needs of a specific department or program. Statistics and figures should be gathered appropriately, but it is good to always be prepared to temper the statistics with qualitative judgments. The required information could even go so far as to include notes taken by liaisons regarding the needs of a given faculty member or department and how the library might seek or have sought to address them. For example, notes for a business department liaison might have something such as "more industry information needed" along with notes about acquiring access to IBISWorld or some other relevant database or resource. The most important thing to keep in mind with an accreditation visit is to have all possible documentation available and ready.

Accreditation often requires years of work as deans and provosts seek in advance to gather information, evaluate programs, meet with necessary department heads and staff, and make any adjustments ahead of the visit, as deemed necessary. That said, an accreditation visit itself tends to be a fairly quick and intense event lasting just a handful of days. The visiting team usually comes in and "sets up shop" someplace on campus. The highest level of administration will place the library and its staff on notice and share the schedule of the visiting team. For example, the University of Waterloo's job description for a library liaison states, "The Librarian works with academic departments in preparing documentation for program assessment and accreditation and may meet with external consultants during review processes."[23] Library administrators and liaisons may be asked to meet with the committee or a specific committee member one-on-one for an hour or more. These sessions tend to be sit-down discussions that involve the opportunity to share what the library staff are doing and to answer any questions the visiting team or team members may have. If an answer to a given question is not available, it is usually acceptable to just make a note and get back to the accreditation team at a later time. When an accreditation team is visiting, all liaisons should be prepared with information even if not scheduled as part of the review process. Often liaisons are called upon at a moment's notice during an accreditation visit to provide supplementary information. If scheduled to engage in discussion with the visiting team, library liaisons should be forthright about any shortcomings or challenges faced by the liaison program. However, they should also seek to share positive efforts to connect the library with external constituencies and meet the needs of its users. It almost goes without saying, but professional attire and demeanor are a must for any such visit. The accreditation visit can be intimidating for new liaisons. However, with careful preparation, the event should go smoothly.

The accreditation team will explore various student learning outcomes in other ways besides talking with library liaisons and reviewing statistics and activities. The team will review material done in the classroom to see if learning standards are actually being implemented and achieved. An example of this comes from a 2010 accreditation report from the City College of San Francisco. Two of the criteria explored were use of multiple sources and integration of the MLA citation style in research papers of the students. To examine this, the accreditation team copied "works cited" pages from student papers in English classes where two-thirds of those reviewed had attended an information literacy class on these topics.[24] Results of this review indicated that the majority used Google search; however, those who attended IL classes did use more of the library resources' credible sources.[25] The recommended action was to increase library research instruction to five hours from one and design a workshop for citing sources.[26] This is a typical example of how an accreditation team will review and examine the educational impact of library liaison activities and make recommendations for improvements.

Accreditation team visits require extensive preparation by the academic institution, including the library and liaison librarians. Records of ongoing statistics on liaison work and activities make these preparations easier. Liaisons should be prepared to explain their support of the educational process regardless of whether they are scheduled to attend the accreditation meetings. Those liaisons attending should come armed with summaries and backup information and be dressed in business attire. The accreditation team wants to be assured that the educational needs of the students are being met. Their visit is a good way for liaison librarians to self-check that recommended standards are in place. While often dreaded, accreditation meetings should be embraced as an objective review of liaison activities, strengths, and weaknesses.

Accreditation Visit Checklist

- ☐ Prepare a summary of liaison work completed and under way
- ☐ Prepare an electronic folder and printed version of liaison statistics
- ☐ Dress in business attire
- ☐ Speak openly and frankly with the visitation team about any challenges and successes
- ☐ Follow up with the visiting team regarding any unanswered questions

New Courses

Perhaps the most critical time for a library liaison in a variety of ways is when new programs are both under consideration and being implemented. In the initial exploratory phase of a new program, consideration at an institution of key individuals sometimes leaves out the library. The liaison can play a critical role in bridging this gap. Either through formal representation on a relevant planning committee or group or by informally inserting oneself in the process, a liaison's role is to carefully consider the potential needs of any program being discussed for addition. Sometimes an institution that has a more formalized role for liaisons will include them in this process automatically. More often than not, however, this may require that the liaison seek out a senior administrator in the library or within a given academic department and request to be included. Networking with these administrators in some fashion would be a critical component in this regard.

The liaison can also advocate for appropriately supportive library resources. Indeed, sometimes even the addition of just one class to a given curriculum can create the need for new information resources. The accrediting and professional standards explored earlier as they relate to a given area usually come into play. Additionally, a comparative exploration of collections at other similar or exemplary institutions that have the same course or program can be done to determine what could be added to the collection. The liaison would then play an important role in working with the library administration to inform the institution's overall administration what the program needs might be one year or even five years down the line.

One of the main areas that creation of a new course will affect is collection development. First, the library liaison must have an awareness of the current collection and resource possibilities. There are countless ways for a library liaison to explore and assess a library's collections. In a smaller library or with smaller programs, it is often easier to have meaningful discussions with most or all faculty. In a larger library, this may not be the case, and, therefore, specific faculty might be targeted for discussions regarding classes and resource needs. The importance of this has already been laid out in this book. Establishing those relationships will lead to faculty who are more communicative about their specific information requirements.

Another key factor is determining what types of resources might best suit students' needs. As previously stated, faculty can often go a long way toward

helping the liaison understand that, for example, databases are more important than books or vice versa in a given course or discipline. The liaisons
themselves, however, must also consider the possibility that faculty in a
given area may not be aware of a change in resources. The most glaring recent
example would be the shift in many libraries from having physical DVD collections to a greater emphasis on access to streaming video. Collection comparison with other institutions that have implemented similar courses is also
a good idea. The liaison has the challenging task of scouring the environment
for new ideas and resources such as these, understanding and considering
the various ways in which they might be used, and then sharing their availability with relevant faculty.

New course development is also a good time to discuss resource funding.
The liaison librarian must of course be familiar with what financial or other
resources are currently available and what might be available to fill any gap
that may exist. For example, how has the library allocated funding in the
past and how might this relate to the area the liaison hopes to serve? It is
important to note that resources need to grow as well in other ways as students progress through many program areas or degrees. For example, a student studying business administration toward a bachelor's degree will have
different potential needs than will a student who is pursuing an associate's
degree. Graduate programs are particularly needy in this regard compared
to their undergraduate counterparts. They often need an institution to ramp
up not only collections but services as well. The interlibrary loan needs, for
example, of an undergraduate who requires an article on global warming may
be nonexistent, whereas a graduate student doing research on climate change
as part of a doctoral dissertation could potentially create much higher expectations from students and faculty. Again, the liaison is there to discern what
those resource and financial needs might be, make recommendations, and
take actions accordingly as new programs and courses are added.

Finally, a review of relevant accreditation standards as they relate to the
new course should be completed. While some of these standards may be the
same as existing criteria, often new courses require expanded resources. For
example, if a new class on photography color and composition is being considered, library resources may include articles on composition, Photoshop
software, Adobe Creative Suite software, and books on photography equipment. If these resources are not available, funds must be allocated to improve
the collection and services. When discussing resources for new courses,

checking with the overseeing bodies of accreditation for requirements will assist liaison librarians in their recommendations. An understanding of the level of service required for a new program is essential.

When new courses are being discussed and developed, liaison librarians must find a way to become engaged in the conversation. Whether through their library director or committee representative or through informal representation, this involvement is critical for libraries to match resources with new course needs. The liaison librarian should explore what resources are needed through faculty, students, other campus collections, and campus course resources comparisons. Additionally, the liaison librarian must have an understanding of the current collection and financial status. The opportunity for funding of library resources to match new course development cannot be overlooked. This, tied with a review of subject-relevant accreditation standards, will allow the liaison librarian to play a relevant role in course development and matching library support.

New Courses Checklist

- ☐ Participation in new program creation
- ☐ Resource allocation financial advocate
- ☐ Collection comparison with other institutions
- ☐ Relevant accreditation standards

Conclusion

Library liaisons need to be familiar with the structure and purpose of accreditation bodies that affect their educational institution. The specifics of the accreditation process followed at their institution should be explored when preparing for a site visit by the accreditation team. Library liaisons must also be familiar with the appropriate standards created by relevant library associations, accrediting bodies, and specialized accrediting organizations as these apply to their specific programs on a regular basis. Records and activities of the liaisons should be kept for accreditation visits, where they are summarized and consolidated for presentation to the visiting accreditation team. Additionally, special attention must be paid by the liaisons when new programs and courses are added. Since the library is not always considered early on in this process, it is often necessary for liaisons to be proactive in preparing for the addition of new programs. With both accreditation and new course development, the librarian's role is to develop methods of supporting the educational needs, implementing library services to enhance course learning, and meeting the appropriate accreditation standards.

NOTES

1. Jane V. Wellman, "Recognition of Accreditation Organizations," *Council for Higher Education Accreditation*, January 1998, www.chea.org/pdf/RecognitionWellman _Jan1998.pdf: 3.

2. Prudence W. Dalrymple, "Understanding Accreditation: The Librarian's Role in Educational Evaluation," *portal: Librarians and the Academy* 1, no. 1 (2001): 28.

3. Wellman, "Recognition of Accreditation Organizations," 4.

4. Ibid., 3.

5. "CHEA at a Glance," *Council for Higher Education Accreditation*, www.chea.org/pdf/ chea_glance_2006.pdf.

6. Ibid.

7. American Library Association, "Accreditation," *Association of College and Research Libraries*, www.ala.org/acrl/issues/infolit/standards/accred/accreditation.

8. U.S. Department of Education, "Regional and National Institutional Accrediting Agencies," *Ed.gov*, www2.ed.gov/admins/finaid/accred/accreditation_pg6.html.

9. U.S. Department of Education, "Accrediting Agencies Recognized for Title IX Purposes," *Ed.gov*, www2.ed.gov/admins/finaid/accred/accreditation_pg9.html.

10. Kelly Field, "Undercover Probe Finds Lax Economic Standards at Some For-Profit Colleges," *Chronicle of Higher Education*, November 22, 2011, http://chronicle.com/ article/Undercover-Probe-Finds-Lax/129881/.

11. "Accreditation," *International Council on Hotel, Restaurant, and Institutional Education*, www.chrie.org/about/accreditation/index.aspx.

12. "Why Accreditation Matters," *Accreditation Board for Engineering and Technology*, www.abet.org/why-accreditation-matters/.

13. "AACSB Accredited," *Association to Advance Collegiate Schools of Business*, www .aacsb.edu/aacsb-accredited/.

14. New England Association of Schools and Colleges, "Standards for Accreditation: New England Association of Schools and Colleges: Commission on Institutions of Higher Education," *Commission on Institutions of Higher Education*, http://cihe.neasc.org/ standards_policies/standards/standards_html_version.

15. SACS College Delegate Assembly, "The Principles of Accreditation: Foundations for Quality Enhancement," *Southern Association of Colleges and Schools Commission on Colleges*, http://sacscoc.org/pdf/2012PrinciplesOfAcreditation.pdf.

16. American Library Association, "Accreditation," *Association of College and Research Libraries*, last updated June 2011, www.ala.org/acrl/issues/infolit/standards/accred/accreditation.

17. Ibid.

18. American Library Association, "Standards for Libraries in Higher Education," *Association of College and Research Libraries*, www.ala.org/acrl/standards/standardslibraries.

19. American Library Association, "Preparing for Accreditation: An Introduction for Librarians," *Association of College and Research Libraries*, www.ala.org/acrl/onlinelearning/elearning/courses/accrediation.

20. "Criteria for Accrediting Engineering Programs, 2012–2013," *Accreditation Board for Engineering and Technology*, www.abet.org/engineering-criteria-2012-2013/.

21. "Handbook of Accreditation," *Accreditation Commission for Programs in Hospitality Administration*, www.acpha-cahm.org/forms/acpha/acphahandbook04.pdf.

22. "Accreditation Commissions," *International Council on Hotel, Restaurant, and Institutional Education*, www.chrie.org/about/accreditation/accreditation-commissions/index.aspx.

23. "Human Resources: Liaison Librarian," *University of Waterloo*, www.hr.uwaterloo.ca/.jd/00001002.html.

24. "Accreditation Follow-Up Report," *City College of San Francisco*, www.ccsf.edu/Offices/Research_Planning/pdf/AccreditationFollowUpReport2010.pdf: 36.

25. Ibid.

26. Ibid.

Evaluation

Having successfully implemented all of the aspects of the liaison activities, the program is now moving forward. Liaisons have connected, communicated, and assisted both faculty and students in areas of information literacy, online support, embedded librarianship, collection assessments, and collection de-velopment. However, while this is a solid foundation, liaison librarians will also have to implement evaluations and make changes to these activities as they move forward. The liaison program will grow and improve only with feedback. There is no guessing at whether communication with faculty is working or information literacy classes are actually meeting the needs of students. Liaisons need to collect real data and opinions to review, revise, and improve these activities. Do not be tempted to skip evaluating the liaison program! This is *very* important. It is not a reflection of personal liaison librarian weaknesses but should be viewed as a tool for making the liaison program the best it can be. Liaisons must plan, implement, and utilize a variety of program evaluation methods. Evaluation is a liaison tool.

Evaluation Cycle

As in other aspects of librarianship, a liaison program is cyclical. This simply means that elements of the program will be implemented, reviewed, revised, and applied again on a defined schedule. Through evaluations, feedback assists in a number of areas of the liaison program. These include goal setting, justification of activities, increased effectiveness, value and efficiency, and program achievements. For the individual liaison, evaluations not only help improve services but also can illustrate the work and assistance this individual provides in his or her job. This is especially helpful at times of annual reviews. Departmentally, evaluation feedback can guide the liaison program as a whole in goal setting and assuring positive service impact as the information support specialist for the college or university. At the managerial level, such evaluations can justify long-term purchases and collection development spending and assist with accreditation reviews. They also solidify the importance of the library in the educational workings of the academic environment and its support of the overall college or university mission. This is especially critical today as libraries are increasingly expected to justify expenditures and validate their value. After evaluations are conducted, these various areas will have concrete data and findings upon which sound decisions can be based. Changes and new ideas for the liaison activities often evolve from feedback results. Because this kind of feedback is so vital, liaison program evaluations become even more critical.

Evaluations will be either user or use studies. User studies will be focused on individuals and more behaviorally oriented while use studies target what individuals actually use or do and are typically more objective.[1] For example, a liaison may want to study the faculty perception of the effectiveness of liaisons in communicating with them, and this would be a user study. A use study may examine how many times a class library guide was used for information. Both types of studies are essential for evaluating liaison programs and activities.

When preparing to do any evaluation, the first step is to determine exactly what is to be evaluated. All evaluations should have a purpose or they will not be constructive.[2] Is it the effectiveness of an information literacy class as demonstrated by student work? Are the methods of communication with faculty working in that they are incorporating library services? Are the online information literacy tutorials utilized and improving student learning outcomes? Any number of program attributes can be evaluated. The liaison program evaluations can be the sole focus of a feedback study or they may also be tied in to more general library questionnaires. For example, a specific survey may go out to faculty asking them to rank the importance of various liaison duties. Often a few liaison program questions are scattered within an annual library survey. Sometimes the purpose for liaison evaluation questions is related to the library's strategic plan and goal-setting needs. The importance of such user studies for task refinement and planning has been well documented by Tom D. Wilson.[3] He states that information-seeking behavior is rooted in the organizational climate, individual personalities, planning, and task performance.[4] Each library liaison program will have a slightly different program emphasis and need, so evaluations may differ. Not all academic environments are alike. Some may require more information literacy classes, which may in turn require student feedback. Other organizations may stress instead the use of librarians embedded in online courses, which may result in an embedded resource use study. A liaison program survey should demonstrate the actual value of the liaison librarian or librarians to the institution and student learning, thus justifying any budget allocated to payroll in this area. As a library professional, the liaison must decide exactly what the focus of the evaluation will be.

Once the initial evaluation parameters are set, the sample population (or those who will be involved in the evaluation) must be determined. Is the evaluation only for faculty members involved with liaisons? Is it for a single department or to be distributed campus-wide? Does the sampling need to target students or a particular group of students such as freshmen? Determining *who* will provide feedback and information is tied to *what* information needs to be collected. This in turn may also impact the method of evaluation chosen. Once the sample population is clear, a method of evaluation must be chosen.

For choosing a method for feedback, any number of options is available. These may include data analysis, interviews, focus groups, surveys, observation statistics, or questionnaires.[5] The type of information, the sample population, and available resources should be considered when choosing a method of evaluation. Can a survey be sent out through e-mail lists? Would participants be available to take part in a focus group? Is there available staff to conduct an observation study? The format must be chosen that will provide the best feedback to match the need, or purpose, of the study. Some specific examples of these formats will be reviewed later in this chapter.

Having determined the format, planning must go into the research methods before implementation. What actions will be observed? What kinds of questions will be asked? What information will the survey cover? How will questions be worded? The research methods chosen must provide the answers to the specific purpose of the evaluation. To assist with this, the liaison may want to consult with colleagues or speak to people involved in the area evaluated. Surveys at other institutions or consulting with faculty who have done research should not be discounted. This will provide good feedback on how to organize the specific questions or observations. Depending on the size of the library, an evaluation planning group may need to be formed. Once a question list is generated, one could use a small sample population or other librarians to review it and provide feedback. This test run of the survey should be conducted to catch any errors or poorly written questions. Once the evaluation is thoroughly revised in order to incorporate the necessary elements outlined above, it is ready for implementation.

Implementation of the evaluation may also require some planning. If the evaluation is a survey going out through randomly selected e-mails, communication with the information technology department may be necessary. If feedback from focus groups is required, these must be scheduled at days and times participants are available to attend. For observational data, the best time and place may need to be determined and the staff member implementing the evaluation scheduled free of other duties.

Also to be considered when conducting evaluations is the impact of the responses on the individuals involved. Is every effort being made to protect the identity of participants? Will any feedback given have a negative impact on the sample population? To better understand these consequences of evaluation, liaisons should take the time to certify themselves in human subject research if directly involved in these activities. This is a simple way to learn about the potential impact of such studies on the sample population. The Collaborative Institutional Training Initiative provides this type of training online at https://www.citiprogram.org/default.asp?language=english. It may be necessary to clear any research activities with the college's or university's Institutional Review Board. While some institutions may not have a clear-cut process, others may require clearance when handling student or institutional data. It is always good practice to check first.

Finally, once the data is obtained, it must be reviewed and analyzed. A brief report that includes a summary of the purpose and introduction to the evaluation should be written. The report should also include the methods and results of the survey. Findings should be summarized and provided in data sets or graphs. In the report, the current status should be stated and compared to the findings, and an analysis of strengths and weaknesses should be addressed. If organizational or program goals are impacted by the evaluations, include those in the summary as well. Have the liaison program goals been met? What recommendations can be made? Were there any weaknesses in the survey to correct and improve for next time? The summary report will provide a formal record of the evaluation results. Conclude the report with a final summary statement. The report will be used to refer back to when making changes to the liaison program in the future. This record is also a good reference for budgetary, accreditation, or goal-setting needs.

Depending on the type of evaluation, the frequency of this cycle may change. For example, the library may conduct a survey annually at the end of the year on all library services, including areas of liaison work. Some institutions may survey the faculty at the end of every term. Other evaluations will come at the end of an IL class or after an orientation meeting. The feedback obtained will impact both short-term and long-term planning. A suggested

Evaluation Schedule—Liaison Services

Point-of-Service Evaluations

- Orientation meetings
- Library guide feedback
- IL class evaluations

Semester/Quarterly Evaluations

- Faculty liaison services
- Specific liaison service projects (e.g., research support, increased communication, personalized assistance, online tutorials)
- Information literacy and embedded assistance
- Use of embedded reference links for online courses

Annual Evaluations

- Effectiveness of liaison services to faculty, staff, and students
- Library guide strengths and weaknesses
- Distance learning liaison services impact
- Quantitative usage statistics (e.g., library website visits, IL classes taught, views of an online tutorial)

FIGURE 11.1
Evaluation cycle

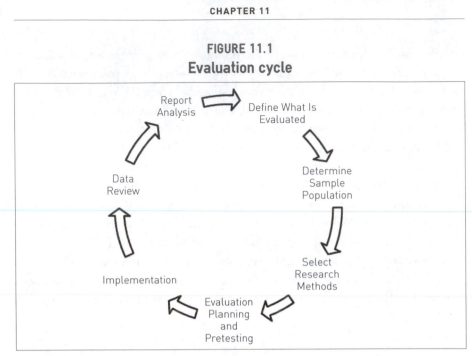

cycle of evaluations impacting liaison duties is illustrated in the sidebar on page 171. Typically, point-of-service evaluations are utilized as needed. While there should always be an annual evaluation covering liaison services, specialized end-of-term evaluations are less frequent and may occur every other year. Having a written evaluation plan provides consistent feedback over time even as administration and staff may come and go.

The completed cycle (figure 11.1) of evaluation methods should give the liaison librarian good feedback. Liaisons should remember to keep the focus of the evaluation narrow and use a test run to work out bugs before implementation. Finally, while it may not be the most exciting part of the cycle, write the analysis of findings and keep for future reference. With these basic steps, along with an evaluation schedule, valuable feedback will be achieved.

Evaluation Cycle Checklist

☐ Determine what is evaluated
☐ Define sample population
☐ Choose evaluation format
☐ Select implementation methods
☐ Write summary report

Conducting Evaluations

The liaison program should be evaluated in two types of areas—qualitative and quantitative. Quantitative data (determined through use studies) is statistically driven and easier to define. This may be the number of information literacy classes taught in a semester. Qualitative evaluations (determined through user studies) provide information on the effectiveness of the liaison program. For example, do the basic information literacy classes improve research skills? Both methods provide liaisons with feedback needed to improve their communications, programs, and other activities.

Quantitative evaluations, because they deal with numbers, are easier to obtain and as a result more common. This type of data can be frequency counts, rankings, scores, or some other measurable number. What types of things can be quantified in liaison programs? The following is a sample list:

- Number of information literacy classes
- Number of students attending information literacy classes
- Number of visits to library guides
- Number of views of an embedded tutorial
- Faculty ranking of the importance of liaison duties
- Number of faculty training sessions
- Number of views of course resource links
- Number of faculty meetings attended by liaisons

Information for quantitative feedback is often readily available if statistical counts are kept by the library. If these counts are not being kept, the liaisons should initiate a program to track activities. Once secured, liaisons need to review this statistical information and determine which of their activities are effective and which are not. For example, if embedded links on a class web page are not being used, what is the reason? Are they clearly labeled? Located well? Are the links meaningful to the student? In another example, improving the number of information literacy classes may be a strategic goal of the library. Liaisons tracking this information may need to strategize how to increase participation. Do they need to reach out in different ways to the faculty? Is the importance of information literacy understood by the academic community? Would liaisons presenting in the classroom versus classes coming to the library help improve numbers? At the J. Murray Atkins Library at the University of North Carolina at Charlotte, librarians analyze annual counts of the number of web courses with library skills, visits to library resources page, informational literacy classes given, and the number of students taught in order to set liaison program goals.[6] A survey used by Texas A&M's library that ranked the importance of liaison services revealed a specific need for faculty education of their available services.[7] These are just a few examples of the ways quantitative evaluations can be helpful to liaison librarians.

Qualitative information will be slightly more challenging to acquire as it cannot be easily measured. Historically libraries had relied more on quantitative data but have shifted much more toward qualitative data in recent years as the focus has turned toward information literacy and student learning outcomes. Qualitative evaluations or methods may involve interviews, observations, surveys, or focus groups. Samples of some aspects for qualitative evaluations in a liaison program are listed below:

- Faculty satisfaction with information literacy classes
- Student satisfaction with information literacy classes
- Effectiveness of an embedded liaison program
- Ease of use of library guides
- Usability of embedded resource tools and links
- Effectiveness of liaisons as educators
- Value of information literacy quizzes
- The impact of the liaison program on student learning

In the example of library guides, feedback on their ease of use may indicate they are unclear, hard to find, or poorly formatted. Are there links to the guides from the home page? Are the guides organized for ease of use? In another example, liaisons may find through qualitative feedback that they are perceived by faculty as poor educators. Librarians can then focus on reasons for this and improve upon either the quality of instruction or the perception by faculty. Are the librarians weak in presentation skills? Do the faculty members feel threatened by librarians in the classroom? At the University of Illinois at Chicago's Library of Health Sciences, a faculty survey was conducted for an evaluation on their online tutorials.[8] The faculty provided feedback on content, composition, marketing techniques, and alternative topics that gave librarians critical information to improve their online learning assistance.[9] A Rutgers University group conducted a faculty survey in 2002 that ranked the importance of various liaison services and allowed liaison librarians to see which activities were more valued by the teaching staff.[10] These types of qualitative evaluations provided necessary feedback for liaison program improvements.

For both qualitative and quantitative evaluations, defining the purpose is still critical. What exactly is being evaluated? Quantitative evaluations are better suited to a survey method. For qualitative evaluations, such as determining the value of the liaison program to teaching and learning, the feedback may be best obtained through a series of focus groups or interviews among the faculty members. Care must be taken to keep information obtained from the interviewees confidential. It is helpful to write down one or two reasons for the evaluation to clearly outline the goals. For example, communication methods with faculty may be the focus of a survey. More specifically, the purpose of a study may be to explore ways to increase liaison-faculty communications in order to incorporate information literacy into classroom assignments. In this case, the faculty members would be the target population and a survey link to questions through an online survey source could be sent. SurveyMonkey is one such service that is available for free (with limited reporting tools) on the Internet. As another example, a qualitative evaluation through interviews may provide feedback on the effectiveness of information literacy class content. The purpose may be to improve the coverage or retention of information in these classes in order to increase the usage of library guides and embedded research links. Whatever the purpose, it must be clearly defined.

Once these parameters are set, survey questions should be created and reviewed by a sample group and fellow librarians. In the communication methods focus, a sample quantitative survey for faculty may contain these questions:

1. How frequently do you communicate with your liaison librarian?
   - Once a week
   - Several times a week
   - One to two times a month
   - Never
2. Select your preferred method of communication with liaisons from the list below.
   - In person
   - Telephone

- E-mail
- Chat
- Skype
- Facebook/Twitter

3. How would you prefer to hear news and updates from liaison
   librarians? (Mark all that apply.)
   - Departmental meetings
   - Library newsletter
   - Library website
   - Faculty web page
   - Office meeting
   - Lunch/coffee gathering
   - Social media
   - Blog

4. Do you use the online collection development form?
   - Yes
   - No

Possible questions to ask to obtain qualitative feedback from faculty might
include these:

1. Are the steps to reaching library guides and research links clearly
   explained?
2. Is the usefulness of library guides conveyed to the class in an
   effective manner?
3. How could the effectiveness of teaching the use of good research
   sources in IL classes be improved?
4. Are the research examples used in the information literacy class
   effective?
5. If you responded yes to question #4, how can they be improved?

As mentioned, before sending the survey out or conducting the focus group
discussions, have the questions reviewed by a small sample group or fellow
librarians. Make corrections to any weak or unclear areas of the evaluation.
This step will improve the effectiveness of the questions in providing feedback specific to the evaluation's purpose. These are only samples of types of
survey questions that can be created. Depending on the situation, these questions will be unique to each academic library.

When planning this implementation of the evaluation, keep in mind some informal timelines in the academic community. Breaks such as toward the end of a quarter or semester (as long as the evaluation avoids end-of-term grading) are natural times to conduct evaluations. Take care to avoid times when students and faculty are not all on campus, such as spring breaks or summer session. If the evaluation involves talking with a focus group or conducting interviews, set up days and times well in advance. This allows participants to clear time in their schedules. (Be sure to offer times that are not in conflict with classes if faculty members are involved.) For observation analysis, pick a time that allows for good feedback. For example, at the Campus Library serving both the University of Washington–Bothell and Cascadia Community College, if part of the observation is determining if students are following along on assigned computers with an information literacy class versus using the Internet for nonclass functions, identifying the place and time is critical. If it is an e-mail survey, SurveyMonkey suggests that Monday offers the most frequent response rate for internal surveys and Tuesday can be included (although not quite as good) for customer or student surveys.[11] Be sure to set start and stop dates for all evaluations and schedule a second request for electronically distributed surveys to facilitate responses. Feedback for individual information literacy classes or presentations by an embedded liaison may be best solicited at the end of the specific IL session rather than at the end of the semester. Overall, give some thought to the timing of the evaluation for best results.

Once the data and feedback are received and the survey or interview ends, the information is reviewed and compiled into a final report. As previously indicated, it is here that analysis of the data and recommendations can be made. Consolidating a wide range of responses will take time. This final report should contain an introduction of the organization and give a brief overview of its status at the time of the evaluations.[12] Next, methods including sample size, process, and questions should be noted.[13] The analysis with recommendations can be made before a concluding summary statement caps the report.[14] The goal is to determine how things are currently perceived or utilized and what changes, if any, can be made to improve the liaison program. It is also good to analyze the effectiveness of the evaluation methods and suggest changes for future studies.[15] Keep this report and use it to make changes and plans for future activities.

Qualitative and quantitative evaluations of both the liaison program in general as well as specific aspects of the program must be done regularly. If possible, make sure these evaluation requirements are noted in the library's strategic plan. Based on the focus of the evaluation, determine a survey method and design questions. As Danny Wallace and Connie Fleet note in their book *Library Evaluation: A Case Study and Can-Do Guide*, evaluations one by one create a "culture of evaluation" that leads to positive impacts on the library.[16] Make evaluation a part of the liaison program!

Conducting Evaluations Checklist

☐ Quantitative feedback
☐ Qualitative feedback
☐ Determining survey methods
☐ Implementation and timing
☐ Evaluation and summary

Microevaluations

While taking larger samples and surveys is a part of evaluating the liaison program, smaller and simpler feedback should also be incorporated. These microevaluations can provide immediate feedback to liaisons as to whether their efforts are effective. Typically these types of evaluations do not need a formal, written report. Instead the liaisons use the information to make minor adjustments for improved results. Three areas of microevaluations include information literacy classes, online information pages, and special events.

A liaison can receive feedback immediately following an information literacy class through student or peer evaluations. Students can answer a simple online survey, given before the class ends, asking if the goals of the information literacy session were met and if the student feels better skilled at finding and evaluating information. The questionnaire should be short, three or four questions, and take only a few minutes to answer. An even simpler student response can be solicited through the use of clickers. Immediate feedback from an information literacy class can also be received through mobile devices, laptops, or pads as well as through online websites such as Poll Everywhere (polleverywhere.com). Peer evaluation can also be an effective evaluation tool for information literacy classes. Having a fellow librarian sit in and offer feedback about content, pace, and delivery of the information can provide the instructional librarian with informative feedback.

Online web pages can also host microevaluations. For instance, a short survey link could be embedded in an online class to check if the resource links or tutorials are helpful to students. A wiki site (try Wikispaces) could be created to solicit student feedback with regard to a liaison's participation and assistance while embedded online with the class. For those using LibGuides, a survey can be embedded into a guide resource polling the effectiveness of the information. At Johnson & Wales University Library at Charlotte, microevaluations are used on LibGuides to solicit feedback from students. As seen in figure 11.2, a microevaluation is planted within an academic leadership LibGuide to gauge the interest level of students in the areas of leadership assessment, planning, theory, and online learning.[17] The guide creator can then take these responses and adjust guide contents to best suit the needs of the users. All of these types of evaluations are geared toward the effectiveness of online information delivery and can be used to improve in these areas.

Finally, any number of special events can have an evaluation component at the end. These may include faculty orientations, library tours, faculty training sessions, in-service training sessions, or any other form of continuing education that involves library liaison work. At the Campus Library serving the University of Washington–Bothell

FIGURE 11.2

Academic Leadership Libguide with "Cast your vote" evaluation

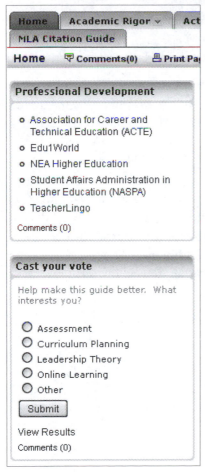

Reprinted with permission.

and Cascadia Community College, the following questions were asked following a faculty orientation.[18]

1. Have you visited the library center before the session?
2. Have you visited the library or media center's web sites before the session, and if so, what for?
3. Have you used the catalog before?
4. What did you find particularly helpful in the session?
5. Was there anything not covered you would have liked to learn about?
6. Do you now feel more comfortable using the library and media center?
7. Would you be interested in an advanced training session?
8. Was the session too long or too short?
9. Was the session held at a convenient time of day, if not, why?[19]

Other evaluation questions may cover the presentation and achievement of learning objectives or offer a Likert scale gauging interest in presented topics. Evaluation questions are not limited but should provide necessary feedback to see if the special event was effective. Whether the survey is delivered on paper or electronically, the number of questions should be limited to encourage feedback.

Feedback can take place in all forms and a variety of formats. Information literacy class evaluations, online web questionnaires, and special event follow-ups are just as important as larger evaluation studies. It is through these microevaluations that various elements of the library liaison's activities can be improved. Liaisons should give consideration to weaving them into their programs.

Microevaluations Checklist

☐ Information literacy class evaluations
☐ Online web page evaluations
☐ Special event evaluations

Conclusion

The use of evaluations is essential to library liaisons. This is not an area for guesswork or gut feeling. It is only through evaluation that real and effective change can be implemented. In the academic environment, its players and needs are constantly changing. Liaisons will be involved in the planning of both quantitative and qualitative evaluations to be implemented through surveys, group interview feedback, and observations. Liaisons also will find good feedback through microevaluations that can be administered quickly and easily on a smaller scale. Because evaluation of the liaison program is cyclical, on a whole it is never ending. To meet this challenge, many major evaluations will be included in strategic plans and the results will affect the future of liaison program activities. Budgets, goals, long-term needs, and program justification, just to name a few, are all affected by evaluation feedback. For the liaison program to thrive, these feedback studies are essential. Liaisons need to be prepared to hear the good and the bad—evaluation is the new best friend!

NOTES

1. Richard E. Rubin, *Foundations of Library and Information Science*, 2nd ed. (New York: Neal-Schuman, 2004), 64–65.

2. Danny P. Wallace and Connie Van Fleet, *Library Evaluation: A Casebook and Can-Do Guide* (Englewood, CO: Greenwood, 2001), 3.

3. David Bawden, "Users, User Studies, and Human Information Behaviour: A Three-Decade Perspective on Tom Wilson's 'On User Studies and Information Needs,'" *Journal of Documentation* 62, no. 6 (2006): 5.

4. Tom D. Wilson, "Recent Trends in User Studies: Action Research and Qualitative Methods," *Information Research* 5, no. 3 (2000), http://informationr.net/ir/5-3/paper76.html.

5. Rubin, *Foundations of Library and Information Science*, 64.

6. J. Murray Atkins Library, "2005–2010 Strategic Plan Template," www.docstoc.com/docs/43094176/2005-2010-Strategic-Plan-Template.

7. Zheng Ye Yang, "University Faculty's Perception of a Library Liaison Program: A Case Study," *Journal of Academic Librarianship* 26, no. 2 (2000): 128.

8. Kristina Appelt and Kimberly Pendell, "Assess and Invest: Faculty Feedback on Library Tutorials," *College & Research Libraries* 71, no. 3 (2010): 245–53.

9. Ibid., 250–51.

10. Tom Glynn and Connie Wu, "New Roles and Opportunities for Academic Library Liaisons: A Survey and Recommendations," *Reference Services Review* 31, no. 2 (2003): 123–27.

11. Jill Zheng, "What Day of the Week Should You Send Your Survey?," http://blog .surveymonkey.com/2011/08/day-of-the-week/.

12. Anthony Chow, "Conducting a Needs Assessment" (online presentation), Library Administration and Management class, University of North Carolina at Greensboro, Greensboro, North Carolina, February 22, 2011.

13. Ibid.

14. Ibid.

15. Wallace and Van Fleet, *Library Evaluation*, 10.

16. Ibid.

17. Johnson & Wales University Library, "Academic Leadership at JWU," Johnson & Wales University LibGuide, http://jwucharlotte.libguides.com/provost?hs=a.

18. Leslie Hurst, "The Special Library on Campus: A Model for Library Orientations Aimed at Academic Administration, Faculty, and Support Staff," *Journal of Academic Librarianship* 29, no. 4 (2003): 234.

19. Ibid.

Conclusion

The more things change, the more they change. The job of the academic library liaison has altered greatly from the bibliographic specialist of the 1940s into its current, diversified role. It is not an understatement to say that academic libraries are in a continual state of modification that appears to be the norm for some time to come. Although the undercurrent of many of these changes is technology, other factors such as staffing, finances, and the future of higher education are also involved. Despite this, librarians still adhere to the core values of providing information access and the encouragement of lifelong learning as the foundation of librarianship. The academic liaisons of today are directly involved in promoting these fundamental principles as they play an ever-increasing role in higher education. The goal of this writing is to give these liaisons a baseline of information for working in this environment and to pinpoint the key areas of understanding needed for this job.

Throughout this book, the importance of relationship building has been emphasized. It is essential for success. The role of initiating, building, and maintaining relationships within the academic sphere continues to grow as a focus for the librarian of today. No longer reticent keepers of information, librarians are required to proactively seek connections and relationships. The new themes of collaboration and knowledge creation force a break from the passive stereotype and a move toward connecting, discovering, and responding. This transforms patrons into people and makes library usage personal. By focusing on relationship building, organizations can uncover new needs and be in position to make a stronger impact. Taking this type of advice to heart, a library liaison forming relationships with faculty and students creates an awareness of academic needs. As noted in this book, the liaison has a special avenue that connects need with service and enhances library use and value.

Technology continues to play a critical role in all aspects of liaison work, and its impact can be found in every chapter of this text. This is especially true as more engagement is needed in course management software. With online classes and MOOCs (Massive Open Online Courses) propagating, the connections widen. As various forms of mobile devices evolve, the library liaison will need to be on the cutting edge of new communication methods. Even while technology changes, the text emphasizes basic concepts of how to utilize this resource, and these ideas can be applied to any future technology product.

The increasing demand on time is another area of change. Although it has already been touched on in several ways, the time needed to be an effective liaison is at a premium. It cannot be overlooked how much this affects the liaison's role. It is the rare librarian who feels as though there is too much time to be had in his or her job, and taking on another duty or role, one which may not even be listed in his or her job description or evaluated during a review, can be daunting. Despite this reality, the prospect of being confined within the library and not making an effort to reach out to faculty and staff appears to be a dead end that leads to a scenario in which the library and the librarians are thought of as unimportant, of low value, or even dispensable. The people who make decisions about the future of the academic library are generally not librarians, and their favorable view of the library and the librarians is of utmost importance.

The future of academic library liaison work will build on its fundamentals and incorporate many necessary adaptations. Exactly what this entails is yet to be known, but there are glimpses ahead. Embedded liaison work has led to classroom integration. In turn, coteaching has blossomed as a new frontier and information technology instruction has begun to find a place of its own in the for-credit classroom. Librarians will become integrated into the learning process and will be found more often in an academic department or class. The liaison's role in an institution's research efforts, in assistance provided to administrators in the accreditation process, and in the assistance provided with course creation will also expand the library's value.

Amid this changing environment, many prospective academic librarians as well as first-year liaisons will struggle meaningfully to establish the fundamentals of their job. In creating this book, our goal was to lay out these tasks of the academic liaison and provide insight on how to perform in each area of importance. This is only a beginning, as each year liaison work morphs and expands. However, the essentials of connecting and communicating, learning a subject area, developing a specialized collection, assisting faculty and students, utilizing technology, and implementing evaluation can be found here. Through this writing, we hope to both assist and inspire new liaisons to embrace their role and the changes to come. After all, fall brings the arrival of a new academic semester, and the time to get ready is now!

About the Authors

JO HENRY received her MLIS from the University of North Carolina at Greensboro in 2011 and holds a master of public administration degree from Georgia Southern University. She is currently the information services librarian at South Piedmont Community College. Formerly, she worked at Charlotte Mecklenburg Library and has over twenty years of experience in sports club management and instruction. Ms. Henry has published in *Public Services Quarterly* and *Library Review* and has presented at the Metrolina Information Literacy Conference and the North Carolina Library Association Conference. She serves as treasurer of the Metrolina Library Association. In addition to her shared authorship of *Fundamentals for the Academic Liaison,* Jo is also coauthor of a forthcoming ALA Editions book on personal librarianship.

JOE ESHLEMAN received his MLIS from the University of North Carolina at Greensboro in 2007. He has been the instruction librarian at Johnson & Wales University Library-Charlotte since 2008, where he has taught numerous library instruction sessions. Before becoming a librarian, he was a systems administrator at Nucor Steel and an IT director at the science museum Discovery Place, both located in Charlotte. Mr. Eshleman completed the

Association of College & Research Libraries Immersion Program in 2009, an intensive schedule of training and education for instruction librarians. He has presented on numerous occasions including at the American Library Association Conference, the Lilly Education Conference, and the Teaching Professor Technology Conference. In addition to his shared authorship of *Fundamentals for the Academic Liaison,* Joe is also coauthor of a forthcoming ALA Editions book on personal librarianship.

RICHARD J. MONIZ JR. received his master's degree in history in 1996 from Rhode Island College and his master's degree in library and information studies in 1997 from the University of Rhode Island. He was awarded a doctorate in higher education from Florida International University in 2006. He has been a director of library services for Johnson & Wales University since 1997 (in North Miami from 1997–2004 and in Charlotte from 2004 to the present). Richard has also, in the past, simultaneously served as head of information technology services and taught classes, including Introduction to Computers, Microcomputer Applications, World History, U.S. History, and American Government. Richard has taught courses for the MLIS program at the University of North Carolina at Greensboro since 2006, including Information Sources and Services, Special Libraries, Library Administration, Information Sources in the Professions, and Online Bibliographic Information Retrieval. He is widely published and is sole author of the 2010 textbook *Practical and Effective Management of Libraries.* Actively engaged in the profession, he has held a number of committee and board responsibilities within ALA LLAMA, ACRL CLS, and Metrolina Library Association. He is also active in non-library organizations such as Carolina Raptor Center, Charlotte Museum of History, and Charlotte's Arts & Science Council, and has given several presentations related to his involvement with these organizations. In addition to his shared authorship of *Fundamentals for the Academic Liaison,* Richard is also coauthor of a forthcoming ALA Editions book on personal librarianship.

Index

Locators in **bold** refer to boxed material/figures